Who Changed God's Name?

A Practical Guide for a Study of the Name *Yahweh*

James E. Harvey

with study guides by Val Harvey

CROSS BOOKS

CrossBooks™
1663 Liberty Drive
Bloomington, IN 47403
www.crossbooks.com
Phone: 1-866-879-0502

First published by CrossBooks   1/4/2010

ISBN: 978-1-6150-7024-4 (sc)
Library of Congress Control Number: 2009929731

Unless otherwise noted, all Scripture quotations are from the Holman Christian Standard Bible

Printed in the United States of America
Bloomington, Indiana

This book is printed on acid-free paper.

Dedicated to Val

My dear wife and loyal companion:
without her encouragement and counsel
this book would not have been written.

Contents

Part Three
New Testament Names

Introduction

My interest in the subject of God's name began several years ago when I was asked to teach a course for Williamson Christian College entitled *The History of the Israelite Kingdom.* My preparation included a careful study of Moses, the leader whom God used to lead His people out of bondage in Egypt.

Moses's first encounter with God was the "burning bush" experience, where God revealed His name for the first time. I felt led to pursue a more serious study of this event and discovered information that gave me a new insight into the nature of God. My appreciation for who He is and what He desires for us to understand about Him was significantly enhanced.

The personal worship of God has become far more meaningful as the result of coming to know His name. I also have learned to apply His name to all the various needs of my life and the life needs of those whom I serve as a pastor.

For some time I have had a growing conviction that this information needed to be made available in a simple, usable form. This book is an attempt to meet that need.

As you begin reading this material, you will find a rather brief explanation of the origin and meaning of God's name from the original Hebrew language roots. Next we examine the unfortunate process by which this original name was changed to a word that has no meaning. Part Two will focus on those combination names that give practical help to every situation faced in human experience. Part Three helps us have a greater appreciation for our Savior's name.

My prayer is that every reader will be helped, as I have been, by this brief study, and that God will be glorified by the revelation of who He is and what He wants to mean to His people.

O for a thousand tongues to sing my great Redeemer's praise,
The glories of my God and King, the triumphs of His grace.

My gracious Master and my God, assist me to proclaim,
To spread thro' all the earth abroad the honors of Thy name.

—Charles Wesley (1707–1788)

Suggestions for the Use of Study Guides

Each chapter of this book ends with a series of study guides. A simple format is followed based on Moses's experience at the burning bush where God first revealed His name. (Read Exodus 3:1–15.)

These segments of study are recommended:

For Part One and Part Two:

- *Standing at the Bush* (a focus on the student's personal need)
- *Seeing at the Bush* (discovering more about God)
- *Sharing from the Bush* (facing the challenge of passing these truths on to others)

For Part Three:

- B—(Basic truth about Jesus)
- U—(Using the truth about Jesus)
- S—(Searching for more truth about Jesus)
- H—(Honoring the truth about Jesus through prayer)

A variety of approaches may be followed in the study of this textbook:

- Individuals who read this material may gain further understanding by working through the recommended study guides.
- Members of a small group study will profit by discussing each suggested help, giving members the opportunity to share answers as well as ask additional questions.
- Those in a retreat setting or Bible conference also may find these guides useful.

All Scripture quotations are from the Holman Christian Standard Bible unless otherwise indicated. The 2009 edition of this Bible uses *Yahweh* as God's name more than 400 times.

Part One

The Importance of God's Name

Chapter One
What's in a Name?

A person's name fascinates me, especially if that name is unusual. Many times when I ask a person the meaning of their name, they reply, "I don't know; I never thought about it." Of course, many parents give names to their children without regard to the meaning. In our culture the meaning of a person's name often is not considered to be of importance.

As a seminary student, I began the interesting study of Hebrew and Greek, the original biblical languages. One very interesting discovery was that my name *James* is the Greek form of the Hebrew name *Jacob* and means "a deceiver." When I shared this information with my mother, she was shocked and strongly denied this fact! Obviously, my parents never considered the meaning of the name they chose for me; they simply liked this name. I followed their example and gave my son the name *James*; and he named his son *James* (hopefully, we will not prove to be a family of deceivers!).

When the Bible was written, most names had significant meanings—meanings that often revealed something about the nature and character of the person. For example, the name *Abraham* means "father of a multitude," while David's name means "beloved." *Matthew* means "the gift of Yahweh," and *Martha* means "lady."

The biblical practice of choosing names came from the belief that the name of a person or a place expressed something important. To know a person's name was to know the person's character or destiny. Parents often choose a particular name for their child to express their hopes for him or her.

Notice that sometimes a biblical person's name was changed to reflect a change in their life. Jacob's name was changed to *Israel*, meaning "God rules." In the New Testament, an early disciple named *Joseph* ("adding") became known as *Barnabas* ("son of encouragement"). And the list could go on and on.

The point I seek to make is that biblical names were important because they often expressed something about a person. This truth leads me to declare that *no other name is as significant and worthy of knowing as God's name.*

I believe that God gave us the Bible to reveal the truth about Himself, His nature, His character, and His purpose for all creation. His personal name is included in His word to help us understand more about who He is and what He wants to do for us. Years ago I heard this truth: Every name He bears reveals a blessing He shares. And I would add: Every blessing He shares expresses the fact that He cares. God has given us His name because He wants us to know Him and to make Him known to others. How vitally important it is for each of us to discover that name!

Consider several statements about the value of God's name. Let's begin with the model prayer, "Our Father in heaven, Your name be honored as holy" (Matt. 6:9). Notice the third commandment: "Do not misuse the name of the LORD your God, because the LORD will punish anyone who misuses His name" (Deut. 5:11). Many references occur in the Psalms, such as "LORD, our LORD, how magnificent is Your name throughout the earth!" (Ps. 8:1). The writer of Proverbs declared, "The name of the LORD is a strong tower; the righteous run to it and are protected" (Prov. 18:10). Through the prophet Isaiah, the Lord promised, "My people will know My name; there they will know on that day that I am He who says: Here I am" (Isa. 52:6). Our Lord Jesus included this in His prayer to His Father, "I have revealed Your name to the men You gave me from the world" (John 17:6).

Through a concordance study I found more than 500 references to "the name of the Lord." What a powerful testimony this is to the importance given by the author of the Bible to His own name! One student of God's word made this sobering statement: "The expression 'name of God' designates at the same time the whole divine self-presentation by which God in personal presence testifies of Himself—the whole side of the divine nature which is turned toward man" [Gustov F. Oehler, *Theology of the Old Testament* (Minneapolis: Klock and Klock Christian Publishers, 1978, orig. 1873), 125.]

We simply cannot overstate the significance of the name of the only true, living God. Join me as we discover His dramatic disclosure of that name above all names.

Study Guide

Standing at the Bush

- Who gave you your name? What is the meaning of your name?
- If someone asked you, "What is God's name?" how would you answer?

Seeing at the Bush

- Why is knowing God's name a matter of importance?
- In your opinion, what name for God is most commonly used when people pray?

Sharing from the Bush

- How would you share with someone the importance of knowing God's name?
- Using a Bible concordance, locate three references to "the name of the Lord" not used in this chapter.

Chapter Two
What Is God's Name?

One important key in discovering God's name is to recognize the difference between a person's name and words that describe that person. For example, my legal name is *James Earl Harvey*; this is my one and only name. But I also have various titles, such as *son, husband, father, pastor, teacher, friend, neighbor, citizen, Christian, disciple*, and so on. These terms help describe who I am, but they are not my name.

Likewise, God has revealed Himself by one name. There are many combinations of this name, but just one name. In addition, there are many titles, such as *God, Father, Son, Lord, Holy Spirit, Creator, Redeemer, Messiah, Counselor, Shepherd, Judge, Savior, Word, Teacher, Friend, King of kings, Lord of lords*, and on and on. Each of these terms reveals more about Him, but *not one of these is His true name*.

What is this most sacred name? We are indebted to Moses for asking God to tell him His name. You may remember this interesting story, found in the third chapter of Exodus. At the time of this dramatic event Moses had been a fugitive for about forty years. After killing an Egyptian, he fled to the land of Midian where he sought refuge. There he met a priest named Jethro, became a keeper of his sheep, and married his daughter.

The second forty years of Moses's life were spent in this land, far from the luxury he had known as the adopted son of the Pharaoh's daughter. One day Moses had an encounter with God that changed his life forever. He saw a desert bush that was engulfed in flames, but not consumed. As he came near this amazing phenomenon, he was startled to hear a voice telling him to remove his sandals because he was standing on holy ground.

This mysterious speaker identified Himself by saying, "I am the God of your father, the God of Abraham, the God of Isaac, and the God of Jacob" (Ex. 3:6). The Lord went on to reveal His plan to use Moses to deliver His people from bondage to the Egyptians, bringing the Israelites to a new land.

Moses was stunned and told God that He had made a mistake by choosing him for this monumental task. God assured this chosen leader that He would be with him, enabling him to accomplish all He intended. At this point Moses said, "If I go to the Israelites and say to them: The God of your fathers has sent me to you, and they ask me, 'What is His name?' what should I tell them?" God replied to Moses, "I AM WHO I AM. This is what you are to say to the Israelites: I AM has sent me to you." God also said to Moses, "Say this to the Israelites: Yahweh, the God of your father, the God of Abraham, the God of Isaac, and the God of Jacob, has sent me to you. This is My name forever; this is how I am to be remembered in every generation" (Ex. 3:13–15).

Sometime later, after Moses had returned to Egypt and began the long and difficult process of convincing Pharaoh to let the Israelites leave, God spoke to him again: "I am Yahweh. I appeared to Abraham, Isaac, and Jacob as God Almighty, but I did not make My name Yahweh known to them ... I am Yahweh, and I will deliver you from the forced labor of the Egyptians and free you from slavery to them" (Ex. 6:2–6). The rest is history—the amazing story of the emancipation of God's people, just as He promised.

God's name is Yahweh! *Yahweh* is a very special name composed of four Hebrew letters in the original script (יהוה) (Hebrew words are read from right to left.). Since at that time Hebrew was written without vowels, this name in English letters is translated by the four consonants

YHWH, described by biblical scholars as the *Tetragrammaton*, meaning "four letters." This name appears 6,823 times in the Old Testament, occurring in every book except Esther, Ecclesiastes, and the Song of Songs. What a powerful testimony to God's desire to be known by His name!

You will notice that the title of this book is *Who Changed God's Name?* My reason for raising this question is the fact that most translations and commentaries use the term *Jehovah* for God's name, rather than *Yahweh*. For example, in the King James Version, *Jehovah*—rather than *Yahweh*— is found in seven locations; all other references where *Yahweh* occurs are rendered as *LORD*. Allow me to give you a brief history regarding the use of *Jehovah* as the name of God.

Most Hebrew people have maintained a deep reverence for God's name. In fact, in biblical times they actually refused to speak His name for fear of violating such commands as "Do not misuse the name of the LORD your God, because the LORD will punish anyone who misuses His name" (Ex. 20:7), and "Whoever blasphemes the name of the LORD is to be put to death; the whole community must stone him" (Lev. 24:16). The reasonable conclusion of such warnings was to avoid the consequences of misusing God's name by never using it. Thus Hebrew scholars substituted the term *LORD* (all upper case) wherever *YHWH* occurred in the biblical text. They also used "Lord" (lower case) to translate the Hebrew word *adonai* which means "sovereign one."

The original Hebrew language was written as consonants, without vowels; the readers understood the meaning of these words, and then supplied the necessary vowels as they spoke their language. About the seventh century AD a group of Hebrew scholars called *Massoretes* came up with a system of writing Scripture with tiny symbols ("jots and tittles") to indicate vowel sounds. Their purpose was to preserve the proper pronunciation of the Hebrew language. In order to give a more accurate rendition of God's name these scholars used the vowels from *adonai* and placed them within the consonants of *YHWH*, producing a new word, *Jehovah* (the J and V replaced Y and W).

Although this seems very confusing to a modern English reader, these scholars were simply seeking to preserve their language, which they believed to be sacred. However, as a result of these changes, the name for God became a word (*Jehovah*) which is a made-up hybrid term that has no meaning. The ultimate outcome of all these changes is the widely accepted use of *Jehovah* as God's name, rather than *Yahweh*. The desire of this writer, and many others, is to restore the use of the proper name for God. Surely no other name is so deserving of being accurately used.

Listen to this comment found in the *Encyclopedia Britannica:* "Yahweh-the personal name of the God of the Israelites ... The Massoretes, Jewish biblical scholars of the Middle Ages, replaced the vowel signs that had appeared above or beneath the consonants of YHWH with the vowel signs of Adonai or of Elohim. Thus the artificial name Jehovah (YeHoWaH) came into being. Although Christian scholars after the Renaissance and the Reformation periods used the term Jehovah for YHWH, in the 19th and 20th centuries biblical scholars again began to use the form Yahweh, thus this pronunciation of the Tetragrammaton was never really lost. Greek transcriptions also indicate that YHWH should be pronounced Yahweh." (*Encyclopedia Britannica*, [15th edition] vol. 10, "Yahweh," p. 786)

What about the sect called Jehovah's Witnesses? I quote from their own book, *Let Your Name Be Sanctified*, "While inclining to view the pronunciation 'Yahweh' as the more correct way, we have retained the form 'Jehovah' because of people's familiarity with it since the 14h century." In response to this view, I must ask: Is "familiarity" the controlling criteria for determining the proper interpretation of God's Word, especially something as important as God's name?

A respected biblical scholar has written: "A more literal translation of the Hebrew is *Yahweh*; but that is strange sounding to us, and *Jehovah* has come to possess a distinctive value we would be reluctant to forgo." I question the rationale of this writer. We should be committed to maintaining the accuracy of Scripture whether a term is "strange sounding to us" or not.

I have discussed this concern about God's name being changed with several teachers of Hebrew and Old Testament studies. I have been surprised and disappointed by their responses. Although they are very familiar with the biblical background of the name *Yahweh*, they basically agree that the use of *Jehovah* is no big deal. Like the author quoted above, they are comfortable with substituting *Jehovah* for *Yahweh* because it has a long tradition that is widely accepted.

Suppose someone decided to change your name, a name that you cherish; and suppose yours is a name has a significant meaning, one that expresses truth about who you are. Suppose they took the consonants of your name and added different vowels, coming up with a new name that had no meaning. How would you respond? Would you not be offended by such an inconsiderate action?

I am pleased to note the use of *Yahweh* more than 400 times in the 2009 edition of the *Holman Christian Standard Bible*, which is the biblical text used in this document. Thus I strongly recommend this translation for your reading and study. As stated earlier, God's special name, *Yahweh*, occurs over 6,000 times in the Old Testament. None of the other English translations I have surveyed, with the exception of the *Jerusalem Bible*—a 1967 French Catholic version, use *Yahweh*.

My contention is that no English reader will discover the true meaning of God's name by seeing the word *LORD* (all upper case letters)—a word in English that refers to God's sovereignty. The concept of God's sovereignty is properly communicated by translating the Hebrew word *adonai* as "Lord" (lower case)—an accurate translation that occurs some 300 times in the Old Testament. How many readers will know there is a significant difference between *LORD* and *Lord?* The first term translates the Hebrew word for God's name, the other expresses one of the many titles for God, and yet both are spelled exactly the same! I say it's time to return to God's original revelation of himself through a very special name.

Just to reinforce the importance of preserving God's original name, follow me through the remainder of this study. Join me as we examine the various combinations of God's name found in the Old Testament. Then consider the root meaning of Jesus's name, as well as all the claims He made that are based on this name. I believe you will be convinced that God's name, Yahweh, is worth preserving.

Study Guide

Standing at the Bush

- What would motivate you to pursue a study of God's name?
- Why was knowing God's name so important to Moses?

Seeing at the Bush

- Explain how Yahweh's name was changed to Jehovah.
- Why should a Bible student be concerned about this change of God's name?

Sharing from the Bush

- How would you inform a Jehovah's Witness about God's true name?
- When you refer to the name Yahweh, how should you respond to persons who are confused by this name?

Chapter Three
What Does God's Name Mean?

When Moses asked God to tell him His name, God replied, "I AM WHO I AM." The most likely English translation of the word *Yahweh* comes from the Hebrew verb meaning "to be." Another way of saying this is "I am the one who is." In other words, God's name declares that He is the eternal God—the one who always has been, always will be, and always is—in the present.

We humans are bound by time; we think in terms of the past, present, and future. However, God is eternal. He has no past, present, and future—just the eternal now. As the psalmist declared, "from eternity to eternity, You are God" (Ps. 90:2). Thus the best name by which He could choose to make Himself known is *Yahweh*—I AM.

In order to understand more about the significance of this unusual name, let's examine the context in which this name was first revealed. At the burning bush, God declared to Moses that He was the God of Abraham, Isaac, and Jacob. Abraham is known as the first of the Hebrews. He is the first to receive this promise from God: "I will make you into a great nation ... and all the peoples on earth will be blessed through you" (Gen. 12:2–3). Here is an unconditional promise (covenant) God made with Abraham; God repeated this same covenant to Isaac and Jacob. Later another covenant was made with David: "Your house and kingdom will endure before Me forever, and your throne will be established forever"

(2 Sam. 7:16). Included in this amazing promise is the gift of Jesus, who was a descendent of David.

God takes the initiative in making covenants with His people. These agreements are promises of blessings He will bestow. Therefore, included in His name is the concept of a covenant—I AM the God who makes and keeps promises, promises to bless My people.

Now return to Moses at the bush. After assuring Moses that He would be with him, God went on to say, "Go and assemble the elders of Israel and say to them: Yahweh, the God of your fathers ... has appeared to me and said: I have paid close attention to you and to what has been done to you in Egypt. And I have promised you that I will bring you up from the misery of Egypt to ... a land flowing with milk and honey" (Ex. 3:16–17).

God was revealing Himself and His nature through His name to Moses. He was saying that *Yahweh* (I AM) means *I AM whatever you need in order to become all that I want you to be.*

Think of all God included in this promise: First, He worked amazing miracles to convince Pharaoh to let the people leave Egypt. Next came the miracle of crossing the Red Sea, and then the miracle of continual guidance through a cloud by day and a pillar of fire by night. This was followed by the miracle of manna and quail to eat, water from a rock, and ultimately, victory over their enemies; and the list goes on. Whatever was needed, God provided—I AM whatever you need!

I remember an occasion when a pastor said to me, "Do you know what single verse in the Bible gives the entire message of the Bible in one sentence?" After a brief pause, I replied, "John 3:16."

"No," he said, "The answer is Philippians 4:19." He proceeded to quote these words: "My God will supply all your needs according to His riches in glory in Christ Jesus." After thinking about these words, I agreed. God is communicating this wondrous truth to everyone through His word: Whatever any person needs, beginning with salvation, God will graciously provide. And all this provision is made possible through Jesus Christ.

This remarkable fact is the reason God chose the name *Yahweh*—I AM whatever you need. How obvious is the importance of insisting that this name—with such a significant meaning—be used throughout the 6,823 occurrences in the Old Testament. As stated earlier, this special name has been omitted from most English translations of the Bible. Rather than translate the Hebrew name for God (Yahweh), a different word (LORD) with a completely different meaning has been inserted more than 6,800 times! I believe this amounts to changing the original inspired Word of God. Join me in the next part of this study as we consider various combinations of God's name, with the specific needs He supplies.

Study Guide

Standing at the Bush

- What difference does knowing that God is eternal make in your life experience?
- What kinds of promises from God are important to you?

Seeing at the Bush

- How would you describe the meaning of *Yahweh?*
- Read Exodus 3:16–17 and recall some of the ways God's promise was fulfilled.

Sharing from the Bush

- How will others respond when you explain to them the meaning of God's name?
- Make a list of your needs God has graciously met. What are some ways you can share this testimony with others?

Part Two

God's Name and Our Need

Chapter Four

Yahweh Yireh

(yah-WEH yir-EH)

יהוה יראה

The chapters in Part Two will focus our attention on a series of unusual terms in the Hebrew text of the Old Testament. Some of these combinations of *Yahweh* with other words only occur one time. But each expression reveals something specific regarding the provision God is ready to make for every person who places their trust in Yahweh.

The first of these terms is found in Genesis 22, one of the most remarkable chapters of the Bible. Here we find the amazing story of God testing Abraham's faith. The test involved Isaac, Abraham's only son by his wife Sarah. God made a very unusual request of Abraham, "Take your son, your only son Isaac, whom you love, go to the land of Moriah and offer him there as a burnt offering on one of the mountains I will tell you about" (Gen. 22:2).

In order to appreciate the full challenge of this command to Abraham's faith, we must remember that Isaac was the son through whom God's promises regarding future generations would be fulfilled—to slay him would be the end of those promises. But Abraham immediately began the process of obeying God—no questions asked.

Abraham took two of his servants along with Isaac, and also a bundle of split wood, some rope, a knife, and a small pot of burning coals—everything needed to make the sacrifice. On the third day of their journey, they saw Mount Moriah in the distance. A clear expression of Abraham's trust in Yahweh occurred when Abraham told the servants to wait with the donkey, saying, "The boy and I will go over there to worship; then *we'll* come back to you" (Gen. 22:5, emphasis mine). Apparently, Abraham fully believed both he and Isaac would return.

A further affirmation of faith was expressed when Isaac asked, as they journeyed to the mountain, "My father, the fire and the wood are here, but where is the lamb for the burnt offering?" Abraham confidently responded, "God Himself will provide the lamb for the burnt offering, my son" (Gen. 22:7–8). So this father proceeded to prepare for the sacrifice, even to the point of binding Isaac, laying him on the wood, and lifting the knife to slay him. At the last moment, God interrupted this man of obedience by speaking these words, "Do not lay a hand on the boy or do anything to him. For now I know that you fear God, since you have not withheld your only son from Me" (Gen. 22:12).

Isaac's earlier question, "Where is the lamb?" was suddenly answered as Abraham lowered his knife, looked up, and "saw a ram caught by its horns in the thicket." This animal became a substitute on the altar in place of Isaac. "And Abraham named that place The LORD Will Provide" (Gen. 22:14). The Hebrew terms for this name are: *Yahweh Yireh.*

Yireh comes from a word meaning "to see." Thus Yahweh-yireh affirms God's faithfulness to supply what He alone can see in advance will be needed. Another interesting fact is that the English word "provide" is the combination of two Latin words meaning "to see beforehand." When Abraham said, "God Himself will provide the lamb for the burnt offering," he was declaring the fact that God saw the need before it occurred and supplied what was needed at the proper time.

Is there a truth for our learning and God's glory in this term? Absolutely! Here it is: *Yahweh-Yireh* means *I AM the One who sees in advance what is needed and faithfully provides it.* Abraham needed a lamb

22

to sacrifice on his altar—Yahweh Yireh. About 2,000 years later, on this same Mount Moriah, God needed a lamb to make a sacrifice. And Jesus, the Lamb of God, paid the sin debt of all humankind—Yahweh Yireh! Here is a clear and powerfully encouraging example of how God's name communicates the fact that He always meets our needs.

Whatever our life situation may require—Yahweh Yireh. God has given us this expression of truth in order to assure us of His promise: "My God will supply all your needs according to His riches in glory in Christ Jesus" (Phil. 4:19).

Study Guide

Standing at the Bush

- Read Genesis 22. If you were Abraham, how do you think you would have responded to God's command?
- How does a person develop a faith like Abraham's?

Seeing at the Bush

- Yireh comes from a word meaning "to see." What are some virtues God sees in you that please Him?
- Give several examples of how God has provided what you needed. How does this fact strengthen your faith regarding future needs?

Sharing from the Bush

- Name a person who struggles with problems and would be helped by knowing Yahweh Yireh. How can you share this truth with them?
- Write your testimony of how God met your need for a Savior through Jesus, and share this truth with another person.

Chapter Five

Yahweh Rophe

(yah-WEH ro-FEH)

יהוה רפא

The previous name *Yahweh Yireh* assures us that whatever we need, He will be faithful to supply. In order to reinforce this truth, God adds a long list of other combination names that apply to more specific kinds of needs. The first of these is found in Exodus 15:22–26. The story of Moses unfolds as he began leading the nation of Israel into the wilderness.

During the first three days of this wilderness journey, the people used all their supply of water. Then they came to a place where they found water; however, the taste was bitter. Therefore, the people complained to Moses, asking him where they could obtain drinkable water, and they named the place Marah, meaning "bitter." Obviously, the Israelites had forgotten the truth revealed by the name *Yahweh Yireh*. Moses, in response to the people, "cried out to the LORD [Yahweh], and the LORD [Yahweh] showed him a tree. When he threw it into the water, the water became drinkable" (Ex. 15:25).

Notice verse 27, "Then they came to Elim, where there were 12 springs of water and 70 date palms, and they camped there by the waters." When Yahweh meets a need, He does so abundantly—not just one spring, but twelve! This reminds us of Paul's words, "Now to Him who is able to do above and beyond all that we ask or think ..." (Eph. 3:20).

God used this need for water as an opportunity to teach His people a valuable lesson. He said, "If you will carefully obey the LORD your God, do what is right in His eyes, pay attention to His commands, and keep all His statutes, I will not inflict any illness on you I inflicted on the Egyptians. For I am the LORD who heals you" (Ex. 15:26).

The Hebrew words for "I am the LORD who heals you" are *Yahweh Rophe.* The term *rophe* means "heal," "cure," "restore," or "make whole." By using these words, God was revealing Himself as the source of all healing, wholeness, and restoration. This understanding comes from the fact that various forms of *rophe* are used elsewhere in the Old Testament to refer to the healing of the body, mind, soul, land, and even nations.

Consider several other examples of Yahweh's healing. Let's begin with physical healing. The psalmist declared of the LORD, "He forgives all your sin; He heals all your diseases" (Ps. 103:3). We can recall various examples of His healing individuals, such as King Hezekiah who was "terminally ill." After he prayed to the LORD for mercy, the prophet Isaiah was sent to say to him, "This is what the Lord God of your ancestor David says: I have heard your prayer; I have seen your tears. Look, I will heal you ... I will add 15 years to your life" (2 Kings 20:5–6).

One of the first descriptions of the activities of Jesus states, "Jesus was going all over Galilee, teaching in their synagogues, preaching the good news of the kingdom, and healing every disease and sickness among the people" (Matt. 4:23). He quickly gained the reputation of being the "Great Physician."

However, we must remember that all physical healing is temporary; this human body is sentenced to die. Our greatest need for healing is that which brings spiritual wholeness. Yahweh Rophe is most actively and permanently at work in this realm. The Old Testament prophets were very perceptive of this truth and consistently called for the people to seek healing for spiritual needs. Jeremiah was sent with this message from the

LORD: "Return, you faithless children. I will heal your unfaithfulness" (Jer. 3:22). Through Hosea God promised, "I will heal their apostasy; I will freely love them" (Hos. 14:4). The psalmist said of the LORD, "He heals the brokenhearted and binds up their wounds" (Ps. 147:3).

One beautiful example of the healing of the brokenhearted is found in the experience of Naomi. You may recall her story of moving with her husband and two sons from their home in Bethlehem to the land of Moriah. These refugees found relief from famine in this foreign place. Also, both sons were married to Moabite women. Unfortunately, Naomi was left alone when her husband and both sons died.

As the story unfolds, Naomi returned to Bethlehem accompanied by her daughter-in-law Ruth, who refused to leave her. Upon their arrival, the local women greeted Naomi by name. She replied, "Don't call me Naomi [meaning "pleasant"]. Call me Mara, for the Almighty has made me very bitter." Remember how the Israelites named the place of bitter water Marah? "I left full, but the LORD has brought me back empty. Why do you call me Naomi, since the LORD has pronounced judgment on me, and the Almighty has afflicted me?" (Ruth 1:20–21).

In the passing of time, Ruth married Boaz and gave birth to a son. Then the women joined Naomi in celebration, saying to her, "Praise the LORD, who has not left you without a family redeemer today. May his name be famous in Israel. He will renew your life in your old age" (Ruth 4:14–15). Surely this sorrowful woman experienced the healing of her broken heart through Yahweh Rophe.

Jesus began His public ministry by standing in His home synagogue and claiming that these words of Isaiah were fulfilled in Him: "The Spirit of the LORD is upon Me, because He has anointed Me to preach the gospel to the poor. He has sent Me to heal the brokenhearted, to preach deliverance to the captives and recovery of sight to the blind, to set at liberty those who are oppressed, to preach the acceptable year of the LORD" (Luke 4:18–19, NKJV).

The Apostle Peter, in his first epistle, gave us insight into the basic reason Jesus was able to provide spiritual wholeness to others. He wrote, "He Himself bore our sins in His body on the tree, so that, having died to sins, we might live for righteousness; by His wounding you have been healed" (1 Peter 2:24). Notice Peter's reference to "the tree," alluding to the cross. Perhaps Yahweh gave a picture of this when He instructed Moses to cast a "tree" into the bitter water at Marah. All restoration is the result of what happened on the "tree" of Calvary. Our spiritual sickness became His, so that His spiritual wholeness could become ours. We are healed spiritually by Yahweh Rophe.

The healing of broken relationships is another achievement of Yahweh Rophe. This includes every kind of alienation, such as broken marriages, divided families, fractured friendships, divisions among Christians, racial strife, and nations being at war against one another. The ministry of reconciliation begins with Yahweh Rophe and extends through all who know Him. The apostle Paul instructed the Christians at Corinth with these words: "In Christ, God was reconciling the world to Himself ... and has committed the message of reconciliation to us. Therefore, we are ambassadors for Christ; certain that God is appealing through us, we plead on Christ's behalf, 'Be reconciled to God'" (2 Cor. 5:19–20).

How interesting that both Old and New Testaments conclude with references to the healing, restoring ministry of Yahweh. Malachi declared His message in these words, "But for you who fear My name, the sun of righteousness will rise with healing in its wings . . ." (Mal. 4:2). Likewise, the closing chapter of Revelation begins with this: "Then he showed me the river of living water, sparkling like crystal, flowing from the throne of God and of the Lamb down the middle of the broad street of the city. On both sides of the river was the tree of life bearing 12 kinds of fruit, producing its fruit every month. The leaves of the tree are for healing the nations, and there will no longer be any curse" (Rev. 22:13).

As we seek to claim this divine restoration, whether physically, spiritually, or otherwise, we must recall the original context in which

Yahweh Rophe first appears. His promise to heal and restore us to wholeness was based upon His people being obedient to Him (Ex. 15:26). Fortunately, He is gracious and merciful, offering His forgiveness and cleansing when we disobey; but we still must be committed to Him as Lord if we expect to experience His work of healing and restoration. And so remember the One who reveals Himself as *I AM healing, restoring, and making whole.*

The next lesson Israel learned on their wilderness journey affords more help for us. Look at another combination of a name and a need being met.

Study Guide

Standing at the Bush

- Name some personal experiences you would describe as "bitter."
- What should you do when life's bitter experiences come?

Seeing at the Bush

- What does the name *Yahweh Rophe* mean to you?
- List various aspects of life where God's healing, wholeness, and restoration are needed.

Sharing at the Bush

- Think of someone you know who is going through brokenness; how can you help them experience the ministry of Yahweh Rophe?
- When you pray for someone who needs healing, begin praying in the name of Yahweh Rophe.

Chapter Six
Yahweh Nissi
(yah-WEH nis-SEE)

יהוה נסי

Israel's first encounter with an enemy is recorded in Exodus 17. The Amalekites were distant relatives of the Israelites (descendents of Esau) and lived in the region where Moses was leading God's people. Rather than allow these kinsmen to pass through peacefully, the Amalekites chose to attack them.

Moses suddenly became the commanding general of the first Israeli army. His strategy was interesting. He called on Joshua, his second-in-command, to assemble a group of men to engage the enemy in battle. Moses said, "Tomorrow I will stand on the hilltop with God's staff in my hand" (Ex. 17:9). As long as Moses held up this staff (shepherd's rod), Joshua's army prevailed; but when he tired and lowered his hand, the enemy prevailed. Two men, Aaron and Hur, came to Moses's aid, holding up his hands throughout the day. By sundown "Joshua defeated Amalek and his army with the sword" (Ex. 17:13).

Following this victory, "Moses built an altar and named it, The LORD Is My Banner" (Ex. 17:15). The Hebrew words for this name are *Yahweh Nissi*. The term *nissi* also may be translated "ensign" or "standard." This

31

word refers to any kind of visual symbol used, like a modern military flag, to identify the soldiers' object of loyalty. Earlier in Exodus, Moses's staff had been used as a symbol of God's power to part the Red Sea, and more recently to strike the rock and provide water for the people (Ex. 17:6). Now the staff was held up by Moses as a reminder to his army that they were engaged in Yahweh's battle, and that He was their hope of victory.

A very important message is found in this passage. We who have trusted Jesus to save us are now on a journey through this world. Every day we face Satan, a formidable enemy who continually attacks us. Satan cannot have our redeemed spirits, but he is determined to prevent us from living a productive life—one that honors God and is a witness to others of His unconditional love and saving grace.

Just as Yahweh was with His people in their journey through the wilderness, He is with us today and is faithful to provide all we need to overcome the enemy. But even as Israel had to engage the enemy in hand-to-hand combat, so must we. Soldiers of the cross cannot expect God to fight their battles for them.

The apostle Paul gave the best counsel for victory in these words to believers in Ephesus: "Finally, be strengthened by the Lord and by His vast strength. Put on the full armor of God so that you can stand against the tactics of the Devil. For our battle is not against flesh and blood, but against the rulers, against the authorities, against the world powers of this darkness, against the spiritual forces of evil in the heavens" (Eph. 6:10–12). He went on to carefully describe each piece of armor provided by the Lord for this spiritual warfare. The good news is that victory is assured if we follow this wise biblical counsel.

Other writers of Scripture also offer encouraging words regarding spiritual warfare. The apostle John declared, "Whatever has been born of God conquers the world. This is the victory that has conquered the world: our faith. And who is the one who conquers the world but the one who believes that Jesus is the Son of God?" (1 John 5:4–5). Our *nissi*, our banner in spiritual warfare, is not a wooden staff or cloth banner, but

Yahweh Himself. As the apostle stated, "Thanks be to God, who gives us the victory through our Lord Jesus Christ!" (1 Cor. 15:57).

An interesting parallel occurs between Moses's experience at Rephidim and this statement from 1 Corinthians. The first time we meet Joshua is when he led the army to victory over the Amalekites. Likewise, Jesus is our commander-in-chief in spiritual warfare. The names Joshua and Jesus also come from the Hebrew word *Yeshua*, meaning "Yahweh is salvation."

David faced many enemies during his lifetime. One of the most persistent was Saul, who at one time was his friend and admirer. On one occasion, when the Lord rescued David from Saul's attempt to kill him, David composed a beautiful song of testimony and praise. Notice his words: "The LORD lives—may my rock be praised! The God of my salvation is exalted … He frees me from my enemies. You exalt me above my adversaries; You rescue me from violent men. Therefore I will praise You, LORD, among the nations; I will sing about Your name" (Ps. 18:46–49).

What name? *Yahweh Nissi. I AM the One who gives victory!* As we face the enemies to our spiritual well-being, such as those described in Scripture as the world, the flesh, and the devil, our only hope of victory lies in the One who is not only with us, but *in* us. He stands ready to supply all the wisdom and power we need to consistently and persistently overcome. Just as Moses erected an altar and named it *Yahweh Nissi*, so we must establish such an altar as a place of worship in our hearts. By so doing, we are declaring to spiritual enemies that the assurance of victory is firmly rooted in the One who is our banner.

Study Guide

Standing at the Bush

- Name two people who have been your Aaron and Hur.
- How have you provided support for a person under attack?

Seeing at the Bush

- What are some visual symbols of God's power today?
- Read Romans 8:37. How can this truth be applied in your life journey?

Sharing from the Bush

- What are some enemies that may prevent you from sharing your testimony?
- Describe how you may overcome these enemies.

Chapter Seven

Yahweh M'kaddesh

(yah-WEH ma-CAD-esh)

יהוה מקדש

One of the most fundamental and important truths about God is the fact of His holiness. The psalmist declared, "Exalt the LORD [Yahweh] our God; bow in worship at His footstool. He is holy" (Ps. 99:5). The prophet Isaiah was given a special revelation of God when he saw the Lord seated on His throne. Angels were above Him and called out to one another, "Holy, holy, holy is the LORD of Hosts; His glory fills the whole earth" (Isa. 6:1–3). Many other references to God's holiness are found throughout the Scriptures; more than 700 are found in the Old Testament and many more in the New Testament.

The Hebrew root word for holy is *qadash*; the Greek term is *hagios*. Both words convey the idea of someone or something being set apart, separated, dedicated, or consecrated. Various English terms come from this root, such as "holy," "sanctified," "sanctuary," "saint," "hallow," and others. To say that God is holy means He is set apart from all His creation in the sense that He is different—He alone is God, and there is none other like Him. No other is like Him in power—He alone creates something from nothing. No other is like Him in purity—He alone is without sin.

No other is like Him in character—all virtue begins with Him. He is *holy!*

We should not be surprised that God, who is holy, provided a corresponding holiness in His creation. The most significant expression of holiness is seen in His chosen people. Of all the various groups of people on earth, the children of Israel are different, separate in God's sight from all others. Notice these words in that regard: "Moses went up the mountain to God, and the LORD called to him from the mountain: 'This is what you must say to the house of Jacob, and explain to the Israelites: You have seen what I did to the Egyptians and how I carried you on eagles' wings and brought you to Me. Now if you will listen to Me and carefully keep My covenant, you will be My own possession out of all the peoples, although all the earth is Mine, and you will be My kingdom of priests and My holy nation'" (Ex. 19:2–6). The same truth is repeated in these words, again to Israel, "You are a holy people belonging to the LORD your God. The LORD has chosen you to be His special people out of all the peoples on the face of the earth" (Deut. 14:2).

The words "special people" translate to the Hebrew word *segullah;* a term conveying the idea of something being a special treasure among all other possessions. In other words, God declared that His chosen people are a special, holy nation, set apart from all others. Think of all those unique, special provisions God made for Israel. For example, He not only called them a "holy nation," but gave them a holy land and a holy priesthood who wore holy garments and offered holy sacrifices within a holy tabernacle. No other nation has a history similar to Israel; they were set apart, sanctified, and given numerous provisions because of God's sovereign choice—truly God's holy people.

The earliest biblical reference to this concept of holiness is found in Genesis 2:1–2, "So the heavens and the earth and everything in them were completed. By the seventh day, God completed His work that He had done, and He rested on the seventh day from all His work that He had done. God blessed the seventh day and declared it holy, for on it He rested from His work of creation." The Sabbath (rest) day was set apart from the other six days, thus called "holy." Later, we will see how significant this became for Israel.

The New Testament clearly reveals the reason God chose one special group of people—through them He brought a Redeemer who would make a way for all people to be God's holy nation. The Apostle Peter addressed non-Jewish (Gentile) believers in this encouraging manner: "You are a chosen race, a royal priesthood, a holy nation, a people for His possession, so that you may proclaim the praises of the One who called you out of darkness into His marvelous light. Once you were not a people, but now you are God's people" (1 Peter 2:9–10).

If God's people are to be a "holy nation," individuals within that nation must be holy. Indeed, this separateness is God's plan. The book of Leviticus is unique among the sixty-six books of the Bible. As the title suggests, this book describes the work of the Levites, Israel's priests. Much of this interesting material deals with various sacrifices and offerings, feasts, laws, and other actions related to worship. One prominent theme is summed up in the word "holy." Consider this statement: "The LORD spoke to Moses: 'Speak to the entire Israelite community and tell them: Be holy because I, the LORD your God, am holy'" (Lev. 19:1–2).

This command to be holy presents a serious problem for every person. None of us is holy and none of us can become holy without God's intervention. Here is the truth about us: "All have sinned and fall short of the glory of God" (Rom. 3:23). There is absolutely no way for a sinner to make himself or herself holy in God's sight.

So, what must we do? Is there any hope for sinners to satisfy God's requirement of personal holiness? The answer is found in another combination name for God revealed to us in His Word. Give attention to these hope-filled words spoken by Yahweh to Moses: "Consecrate yourselves and be holy, for I am the LORD your God. Keep My statutes and do them; I am the LORD who sets you apart" (Lev. 20:7–8). The last Hebrew words of this command are, *Yahweh M'kaddesh* (I AM the One who sanctifies). This same combination occurs in five other places in Leviticus—21:8, 23; 22:9, 16, and 32.

One writer suggests that of all the names of Yahweh, this one is the most unfamiliar and least known. And yet the truth conveyed by this name is one of the most important. We who are not holy and must become holy can be made holy by Him who alone is holy. Good news! He declares Himself to be the One who is able and willing to make us holy. But how does He accomplish this miracle?

Two basic aspects of holiness or sanctification are introduced. One way of expressing this fact is to say that the first aspect of sanctification is positional, and the second is practical. What does this mean? Positional sanctification occurs the moment a sinner repents of sin, believes the truth about Jesus Christ, and receives Him as Savior-Lord. This decision results in a miracle which is known as being born again, saved, converted, or justified.

Included in this wonder of personal salvation is the believer's possession of the Holy Spirit, the Spirit of Christ. The apostle Paul often referred to this truth. For example, he wrote these words to Timothy, "Hold on to the pattern of sound teaching that you have heard from me, in the faith and love that are in Christ Jesus. Guard, through the Holy Spirit who lives in us, that good thing entrusted to you" (2 Tim. 2:13–14). Again, Paul told the Corinthian believers, "Don't you know that you are God's sanctuary and that the Spirit of God lives in you? If anyone ruins God's sanctuary, God will ruin him; for God's sanctuary is holy and that is what you are" (1 Cor. 3:16–17). And likewise, consider this probing question: "Do you not know that your body is a sanctuary of the Holy Spirit who is in you, whom you have from God? You are not your own, for you were bought at a price; therefore glorify God in your body" (1 Cor. 6:19–20).

Remember, the terms *sanctuary* and *holy* are from the same root word in the Hebrew and Greek languages, with the basic meaning of being "set apart." The presence of God's Holy Spirit in us makes our body a temple, a sanctuary. Therefore, we believers are set apart—holy ones. Another term from the same root is *saint*. Paul addressed several of his letters to "the saints" in various places.

One writer says there are only two kinds of persons in this world—the saints and the ain'ts—those who have the Holy Spirit and those who don't! Positional sanctification refers to the fact that having the Holy Spirit sets us apart from all others; we have the *position* of being sanctified because our body is the temple of the Holy Spirit.

Practical sanctification, on the other hand, refers not to a position but to a process whereby the Holy Spirit is at work in us to produce a lifestyle of holiness. As Paul wrote to the Thessalonian Christians, "This is God's will, your sanctification: that you abstain from sexual immorality, so that each of you knows how to possess his own vessel in sanctification and honor ... for God has not called us to impurity, but to sanctification" (1 Thess. 4:3–8). Again, both the godly character and conduct of one who follows Jesus sets that believer apart from the rest of the world.

The name *Yahweh M'kaddesh* assures us that God is willing and able to accomplish both aspects of sanctification. First, the presence of His Spirit sets us apart in the position of being His temple; and second, the power of His Spirit is faithfully, persistently working to change us into Christ-like people. So in one sense we are sanctified, but in another sense we are being sanctified. Both are due to Yahweh M'Kaddesh.

What is our part in this amazing achievement? The writer of Hebrews expressed our responsibility in this way: "Pursue peace with everyone, and holiness—without which no one will see the Lord" (Heb. 12:14). We are commanded to "pursue" holiness. This imperative means we are to diligently seek to avoid sinful attitudes and actions while focusing on those qualities that accurately reflect the life of Christ.

Paul was very specific about this issue when he wrote: "Put on the new man, the one created according to God's likeness in righteousness and purity of the truth ... put away lying ... . All bitterness, anger and wrath, insult and slander must be removed from you, along with all wickedness. And be kind and compassionate to one another, forgiving one another, just as God also forgave you in Christ. Therefore be imitators of God, as dearly loved children" (Eph. 4:24-5:1).

The importance of our sanctification is revealed by the longest recorded prayer of Jesus. Shortly before He went to the cross He prayed for all who would believe on Him. He included this request of His Father: "Sanctify them by the truth; Your word is truth" (John 17:17). Yahweh M'kaddesh is answering this prayer daily.

Study Guide

Standing at the Bush

- Name several pieces of evidence in your life that indicate a lack of holiness.
- How have you attempted to overcome these shortcomings?

Seeing at the Bush

- What has Yahweh M'Kaddesh done to provide holiness for you?
- Read 1 Peter 2:9–10. How would you paraphrase these verses?

Sharing from the Bush

- State why the following statement is good news to be shared: God declares Himself to be the One who is able and willing to make us holy.
- Write the meaning of positional sanctification and practical sanctification, as discussed in the text.

Chapter Eight
Yahweh Shalom
(yah-WEH sha-LOME)

יהוה שלום

The book of Judges covers a period of approximately 400 years. During this time, Israel was like a flock of sheep without a shepherd. The people had no leader to keep them together. Consequently they strayed from worshiping Yahweh and keeping His commands. One description of their condition is found in these sad words, "After them [those of the generation who followed Joshua] another generation rose up who did not know the LORD or the works He had done for Israel. The Israelites did what was evil in the LORD's sight. They worshiped the Baals and abandoned the LORD, the God of their fathers" (Judg. 2:10–11).

One writer calls the period of the Judges a time of "chaotic restlessness." God sought to help His people by calling out a series of twelve judges; some were good, while others were not. One was a young Israelite named Gideon. Yahweh called him as a young man when he was secretly threshing wheat in order to hide it from the enemy. In response to God's call, Gideon asked for a sign. When Gideon brought an offering of a young goat and unleavened bread, the offering was miraculously consumed by a fire from God. Yahweh spoke to him, saying, "Peace be to you. Don't be afraid, for you will not die. So Gideon built an altar to the LORD there and called it Yahweh Shalom" (Judg. 6:23–24).

Shalom is a Hebrew word extremely rich in meaning. On 170 occasions, *shalom* is translated as "peace." Numerous other times the translation reads "wholeness," "wellness," "completeness," "fulfillment," "health," and "welfare," and is used as the word of greeting when persons meet. If you greeted a Jewish man you would say, "*Shalom aleichem*," meaning "peace be unto you." The proper response would be to reverse the words and say, "*Aleichem shalom*," meaning "unto you be peace." The concept conveyed by this lovely word is that of personal completeness as a result of living in harmony with God.

Another biblical word closely related to *shalom* is *salvation*, a term emphasizing the same wholeness resulting from God's gracious act of delivering a person from sin and sin's consequences. How interesting that the most revered city mentioned in the Bible is Jerusalem, and some sources give the meaning as "possession of peace" (shalom).

Gideon chose to call his altar *Yahweh Shalom*. He understood that the peace so desperately needed by his people would be provided by the One who is the true source of all welfare and prosperity. An altar was a place of worship; Gideon responded to Yahweh's promise by worshiping Him as the giver of peace.

Through this combination name, Yahweh reveals truth about Himself to us. He desires to provide the wholeness of life we need. Consider other references to shalom: "You will keep in perfect peace the mind that is dependent on You, for it is trusting in You" (Isa. 26:3). The words "perfect peace" in Hebrew are "shalom, shalom." Also, "The LORD gives His people strength; the LORD blesses His people with peace" (Ps. 29:11). One of the best known and loved benedictions in the Bible is found in Numbers. On this occasion, the Lord told Moses to instruct Aaron and his sons about the way they were to bless the Israelites in these words:

> The LORD [Yahweh] bless you and protect you;
> The LORD [Yahweh] make His face shine on you,
> And be gracious to you;
> The LORD [Yahweh] look with favor on you
> And give you peace [shalom] (Num. 6:24–26).

The New Testament continues God's promise of peace as revealed in the words of Jesus, the Prince of Peace: "Peace I leave with you. My peace I give to you … your heart must not be troubled or fearful" (John 14:27). He provides this priceless gift through His sacrifice for our sins. Paul said, "Therefore, since we have been declared righteous by faith, we have peace with God through our Lord Jesus Christ … for while we were still helpless, at the appointed moment, Christ died for the ungodly" (Rom. 5:1, 6).

When Jesus first appeared to an assembly of His disciples following His resurrection, He greeted them by saying, "Peace to you!" (John 20:21). If He had been speaking Hebrew, He would have said, "Shalom aleichem." How appropriate was this greeting, because true peace was made available due to His death, burial, and resurrection. This is the peace and wholeness all people long for. We are aware of the quest for peace of mind so widely sought and so seldom found by most people.

One very typical example of the futile search for peace through this world's provisions is seen in the words of a popular song by John Lennon of Beatles fame. His song, "I'm So Tired," has this line: "I'd give you everything I've got for a little peace of mind." He discovered what many others have found—nothing this world offers brings lasting peace of mind.

The good news Jesus came to declare is recorded in these words spoken shortly before He went to the cross, "Peace I leave with you. My peace I give to you. I do not give to you as the world gives. Your heart must not be troubled or fearful" (John 14:27). A short time later He repeated His promise in this statement: "I have told you these things so that in Me you may have peace. You will have suffering in this world. Be courageous! I have conquered the world" (John 16:33).

As a pastor, I have seen many examples of people having peace in spite of extremely troublesome experiences. I recall one occasion regarding a young married couple who were members of the church where I served. The husband was a police officer; the couple had a two-year-old son. One Sunday they went home after church and as his mother prepared lunch, this child went in the garage, found a can of gasoline, and poured it on his toy lawnmower. When the fumes reached the hot water heater, there was an explosion. This precious child died three days later. In the midst of their grief, the parents looked to Jesus for comfort and hope. I conducted the funeral and noticed the father came to the service with his Bible in his hand. This was his source of hope that gave peace. Later the couple had two more children and became leaders in that church. How could this happen? Yahweh Shalom!

Through experiences like these, plus the strong testimony of Scripture, I have come to this strong conviction: Favorable circumstances in life cannot bring peace to those who do not trust Jesus, nor can adverse circumstances destroy the peace of those who know Him as the Prince of Peace.

Study Guide

Standing at the Bush

- Which of these areas of your life is most needful of peace: physical, emotional, spiritual, or social?
- Name some personal results of living in harmony with God.

Seeing at the Bush

- How has Jesus become *Yahweh Shalom* today?
- Compare "shalom" and "salvation."

Sharing from the Bush

- Write a letter to someone explaining the way to peace with God.
- Greet a friend with the word "Shalom," then explain what you mean.

Chapter Nine

Yahweh Tsidkenu

(yah-WEH tsid-KAYnu)

יהוה צדקנו

In order to appreciate the good news of the gospel, we first must be aware of the bad news of our total lack of the one virtue which God requires. The Bible declares that God is righteous, meaning He is without sin. His nature is holy and pure in every aspect. To be acceptable to God, a person must likewise be righteous, without sin.

However, all humankind is unrighteous—totally corrupt. As Paul pointed out in his epistle to the church at Rome (where he is quoting from Psalms 14:1) "There is no one righteous, not even one" (Rom. 3:11). Think about this truth: Even the best person who ever lived, other than Jesus, has in some way sinned against God and therefore is disqualified from a personal relationship with God. Being acceptable to God is literally impossible for all humankind—no exceptions. We all make attempts at being good; we seek to please God in our own ways. But the result of all our efforts to be righteous is accurately described in these graphic words: "All of us have become like something unclean, and all our righteous acts are like a polluted garment" (Isa. 64:6). (A "polluted garment" refers to a menstrual cloth!)

Thus no one can be accepted by God on the basis of his or her own merit. This difference between God and all humanity creates a major problem. Job describes this dilemma in the following question: "How can a person be justified before God?" (Job 9:2). And the psalmist raised the same issue when he asked, "LORD if you considered sins, LORD, who could stand?" (Ps. 130:3). These questions speak of bad news—the worst possible news! Unless we fully appreciate and accept our moral and spiritual disqualification, we are ignorant regarding our destitute and utterly helpless condition.

One of Job's friends, Bildad the Shuhite, asked two of the most important of all questions: "How can a person be justified before God? How can one born of woman be pure? (Job 25:4). Fortunately, God Himself has supplied the answer. As Paul the theologian wrote: "For all have sinned and fall short of the glory of God. They are justified freely by His grace through the redemption that is in Christ Jesus. God presented Him as a propitiation through faith in His blood, to demonstrate His righteousness, because in His restraint God passed over the sins previously committed. He presented Him to demonstrate His righteousness at the present time, so that He would be righteous and declare righteous the one who has faith in Jesus" (Rom. 3:23–26). Good news! All who have faith in Jesus are declared righteous—amazing grace!

In spite of our sinful ways and our complete unworthiness of God's mercy, He has chosen to provide for us what He demands from us—righteousness. And this righteousness is more than a declaration of forgiveness; more than the cancellation of our sin debt. God's righteousness is actually a person. His name is *Yahweh Tsidkenu.*

This interesting combination name for God occurs first in Jeremiah 23:5–6. Yahweh spoke to Jeremiah at a time when the people of Judah were about to be carried away to Babylon as captives—a very dark period of history for God's chosen people. Notice these words of hope given to the prophet: "The days are coming—this is the LORD's declaration— when I will raise up a righteous Branch of David. He will reign wisely as king and administer justice and righteousness in the land. In His days

Judah will be saved, and Israel will dwell securely. This is what He will be named: The LORD Is Our Righteousness." In Hebrew this name is *Yahweh Tsidkenu*.

The term *tsidkenu* comes from *tsedek*, which means to be straight, and is translated as "righteousness." The implication is that Yahweh is righteous in the sense of being perfect—One who always acts with justice. The psalmist declared of Him, "The LORD reigns! Let the earth rejoice ... righteousness and justice are the foundation of His throne" (Ps. 97:1–2). The promise given through Jeremiah pointed to the future appearance of a person called "a righteous Branch of David." The fulfillment of this promise came in the person of Jesus, a direct descendent (branch) of King David.

After the most notable Day of Pentecost, when the Holy Spirit was given to all believers, Peter preached to a crowd gathered at the temple. In this inspired message, he boldly declared, "The God of Abraham, Isaac, and Jacob, the God of our fathers, has glorified His Servant Jesus, whom you handed over and denied in the presence of Pilate, when he had decided to release Him. But you denied the Holy and Righteous One, and asked to have a murderer given to you" (Acts 3:13–14). Jesus is identified as "the righteous Branch of David" promised some 600 years earlier through Jeremiah.

As we pointed out earlier, Paul gave the clearest expression to the manner by which we partake of this gift of righteousness. Listen to these encouraging words: "He made the One who did not know sin to be sin for us, so that we might become the righteousness of God in Him" (2 Cor. 5:21). Ponder carefully the wonder of this miracle: We sinners—totally unrighteous and incapable of ever becoming righteous of ourselves—can literally "become the righteousness of God" by simply trusting the Lord Jesus to be our substitute on the cross! His righteousness is imputed to our account, and imparted to us by the presence of His Spirit in our hearts. This truth means that the very righteousness we need is provided as a gift to us. Righteousness is not attained but obtained. Wonder of wonders!

Here is another powerful example of the significance of the combination names of Yahweh. Through these names He continues to reveal more and more of His manifold nature to us. What a pleasure and privilege to appropriate each facet of Yahweh in meeting all our needs.

Now proceed with me to the next name on this inspiring list. These names not only enhance our worship of Yahweh but also equip us to serve Him more effectively.

Study Guide

Standing at the Bush

- How have you made attempts to please God in your own way?
- Why are these attempts inadequate to make you right with God?

Seeing at the Bush

- How has God chosen to provide for us the righteousness He requires?
- What does the name *Yahweh Tsidkenu* mean to you?

Sharing from the Bush

- Share with a friend the prophecy of Jeremiah 23:5–6 and explain what "the Righteous Branch" of David means.
- What would you say to someone who claims to be right with God because of good works?

Chapter Ten
Yahweh Shammah
(yah-WEH SHAM-mah)

יהוה שמה

The single occurrence of this wonder-filled name is found in the final words of the book of Ezekiel. You may recall that Ezekiel lived among the Jewish exiles in Babylon where he was inspired to speak of God's judgment upon Israel. His messages clearly stated that the reason God allowed His people to be taken captive by Babylonians was their rebellion against Him and their turning to the worship of idols.

God's message to His wayward people included hope for the future. The final chapters of Ezekiel's prophesy include the promise of restoration to their original homeland and the rebuilding of the temple. This structure had always been a reminder to God's people that He was present with them. In one of Ezekiel's visions he saw the "glory of the LORD" entering the new temple and heard Him say, "Son of man, this is the place of My throne and the place for the soles of My feet where I will dwell among the Israelites forever" (Ezek. 43:7).

Not only the temple but also a special city was promised in the prophet's visions. And Ezekiel concludes his message with this interesting statement: "The perimeter of the city will be six miles and the name of the city from that day on will be Yahweh Is There [Yahweh Shammah]" (Ezek. 48:35).

One of the unique features of Hebrew religious belief is the fact of Yahweh's presence with His people. Numerous references to this presence can be found throughout the Bible beginning with the story of God coming to Adam and Eve in the garden. Over and over the sacred story speaks of this divine initiative. Throughout the Scriptures a clear revelation is given of the fact that God is not only in heaven but also with His people. The omnipresence of Yahweh is as important to biblical truth as His omniscience and omnipotence. He is not only all-knowing and all-powerful, but also everywhere and always present. Let's examine some of the references to Yahweh's presence and learn from them.

First, consider the experience of Jacob as he was fleeing for his life from the wrath of his brother Esau. During his journey he had a dream in which Yahweh appeared to him and said, "Look, I am with you and will watch over you wherever you go. I will bring you back to this land, for I will not leave you until I have done what I have promised you" (Gen. 28:15–22). In grateful response to the assurance of this promise, Jacob set up a stone marker, anointed it with oil, and named that place Bethel (House of God). This was the first of several such encounters. *Yahweh Shammah!*

Next, recall how Moses faced the awesome task of leading thousands of Israelites through a barren wilderness. Early in this journey he asked Yahweh who He would send to accompany him in this formidable task. Listen to God's reply: "My presence will go with you, and I will give you rest." Moses replied, "If Your presence does not go, don't make us go up from here. How will it be known that I and Your people have found favor in Your sight unless You go with us?" Then Moses made this interesting observation: "I and Your people will be distinguished by this [His presence] from all the other people on the face of the earth" (Ex. 33:14–16). In the opinion of this leader, the presence of Yahweh would set them apart from all other people.

You will remember several clear expressions of Yahweh's presence throughout those forty years—a pillar of cloud by day and fire by night. In addition to this phenomenon was the Tabernacle that housed the Ark of the Covenant with the two angel figures facing one another on top of the mercy seat. Yahweh referred to this most sacred place when He said to Moses, "I will meet with you there above the mercy seat, between the two cherubim that are over the ark of the testimony; I will speak with you from there about all that I command you regarding the Israelites" (Ex. 25: 22). *Yahweh Shammah!*

Perhaps the most memorable expression of Yahweh's inescapable presence is found in David's Psalm 139. With wonder and gratitude he asked Yahweh, "Where can I go to escape Your Spirit? Where can I flee from Your presence? If I go up to heaven, You are there; if I make my bed in Sheol, You are there. If I live at the eastern horizon or settle at the western limits, even there Your hand will lead me; Your right hand will hold on to me" (Psalm 139:7–10). *Yahweh Shammah!*

I want to share a personal testimony at this point. As a university student I became involved with the campus Baptist Student Union. There I had my first opportunities to speak publicly for the Lord. Gradually I became aware of God's call to vocational ministry rather than a career in engineering which I had chosen. One morning my phone rang. A deacon from a nearby small rural church called to invite me to preach at his church; they were looking for a pastor. I knew that I was not ready to serve as a pastor, but I had promised the Lord to go wherever He opened a door. So I agreed to speak the following Sunday.

With much anxiety I began searching the Scripture for help. As I randomly read various passages I came to Isaiah 41. Verse 10 contains this promise: "Do not fear, for I am with you; do not be afraid, for I am your God. I will strengthen you; I will help you; I will hold on to you with My righteous right hand." Immediately I sensed the peace that comes from His promised presence. Many times since that memorable experience I have been comforted by that promise. *Yahweh Shammah!*

(Fortunately, that church recognized my immaturity and did not invite me back!)

Now go with me to the New Testament for the most significant event regarding the presence of Yahweh with His people. The second chapter of Acts records the outpouring of God's Spirit upon His church on the Day of Pentecost. This miracle ushered in a new era in God's work on earth. Previous to this divine invasion, Yahweh's presence with individuals was limited to various times and places. But on this historic day, all believers were literally baptized with and in the Holy Spirit, resulting in His presence within each one—permanently! Nothing like this event had occurred previously.

Jesus had promised this remarkable blessing before His departure. Just a short time before His arrest and crucifixion He spoke these words to His disciples, "If you love Me, you will keep My commandments. And I will ask the Father, and He will give you another Counselor to be with you forever. He is the Spirit of truth. The world is unable to receive Him because it doesn't see Him or know Him. But you do know Him, because He remains with you and will be in you. I will not leave you as orphans; I am coming to you" (John 14:15–18). About fifty days later, this promise was fulfilled, and since that day every true follower of Jesus has received the Holy Spirit at the moment of new birth. He is the Counselor who remains with us forever.

Allow me to conclude this chapter with a very practical suggestion. You may be like many other Christians who often pray like this: "Lord, please *be with me* today." Or you may ask God to *be with* your Bible study class or to *be with* the church worship service. Such a prayer is unnecessary and even expresses a lack of faith in God's promise. He has declared repeatedly, "I am with you always; I will never leave you." Would it not be much better to affirm His promise and His presence by praying, "Lord, thank You that You are with me and will never leave me." *Yahweh Shammah*!

Study Guide

Standing at the Bush

- Describe a time in your life when you felt all alone and needed hope.
- Read Genesis 28:15–22. Explain what this meant to Jacob.

Seeing at the Bush

- How are you comforted by the fact that God is not only in heaven but also with His people?
- Read Psalm 139:7–10. What are two benefits God provides by being always present (*Yahweh Shammah*)?

Sharing from the Bush

- In Acts 2 an exciting event occurred on the Day of Pentecost. Tell a friend what happened.
- How would you share with someone that all true followers of Jesus received the Holy Spirit at the moment of their new birth?

Chapter Eleven
Yahweh Rohi
(yah-WEH row-EE)

יהוה רעי

I've been told there are 1,188 chapters in the Bible. Without question, the best known, best loved, and most remembered of these is Psalm 23. This simple yet profound statement of trust is comprised of only fifty-five Hebrew words, and can easily be read in less than one minute. What makes this brief composition so widely loved and cherished?

Perhaps the answer is found in the opening statement, "The LORD is my shepherd." Those first five words are a translation of the Hebrew words, *Yahweh Rohi*. Here is another combination name of God by which He communicates very significant truths about Himself. Most people in biblical times were well acquainted with an agrarian lifestyle, thus the frequent use of metaphors regarding sowing seed, harvesting grain, tending sheep, raising cattle, keeping orchards, and other farm-related interests.

David, who is believed to be the writer of Psalm 23, grew up tending his father's sheep. Out of his experience as a shepherd, he saw the parallels between the relationship of a shepherd and his sheep and the LORD and His people. In fact, the central theme of this poem is that of personal relationship. Psalm 23 has been called the "He-me Psalm," due to the many uses of these personal pronouns.

This intimacy between the sheep and the Shepherd is the key to all that follows. The text could be phrased, "Because Yahweh is my shepherd ...." Our study of the name Yahweh, and all this sacred name implies, adds greatly to our appreciation of David's testimony here. He is declaring the fact that just as he (David) loved his sheep, and provided for all their needs, Yahweh does the same for him.

One very interesting approach to an exposition of the meaning of Psalm 23 is the use of all the combination names of God we have been studying. Join me as we apply to this psalm what we have learned from these recent chapters.

Verse 1: "The LORD is my shepherd [*Yahweh Rohi*]; there is nothing I lack." David learned from experience that Yahweh always faithfully provided for everything he needed. This provision does not include everything he may have wanted or thought he needed, but that all his actual needs would be provided. This affirmation of faith reminds us of Abraham's experience when he offered up Isaac to the LORD (see Chapter Four). When Yahweh provided a ram to be offered in place of Isaac, Abraham named that place of sacrifice *Yahweh Yireh* (I am the One who provides).

When we turn the management of our lives over to Yahweh, we can give the same testimony David gave. All our needs will be met. He is a Good Shepherd—one who laid down His life for His sheep. Surely He can be trusted to provide all other needs; we will lack nothing.

Verse 2: "He lets me lie down in green pastures; He leads me beside quiet waters." Sheep will not lie down unless they are at peace—plenty of food, safe from enemies, nothing to fear. And they must have a quiet pool of water for drinking, not a swift running stream. This verse paints a lovely picture of peace. The good shepherd understands the needs of his sheep and makes provisions so they can rest peacefully.

Think back to Chapter Eight and our study of Yahweh Shalom (I am peace). Just as a good shepherd gives his sheep the peace of being free from fear, and the freedom to rest quietly, so Yahweh Shalom is our unfailing source of true peace. Remember Jesus's words to His disciples, given at a time of extreme conflict and chaos, "I have told you these things so that in Me you may have peace. You will have suffering in the world. Be courageous! I have conquered the world" (John 16:33). True peace is found only in one person, *Yahweh Shalom.*

Verse 3a: "He renews my life." The Bible compares humankind to sheep more than to any other of God's creatures. One good reason for this selection is that sheep are very dependant on shepherds for their well-being. For example, sheep are prone to wander away from the fold, get lost, and not be able to find their way back. We can recall Isaiah's familiar words: "We all went astray like sheep; we have turned to our own way" (Isa. 53:6). If Yahweh Rohi did not take the initiative in coming after us in our lostness, we could never be saved.

Sheep also have a problem with becoming "cast down." This term is a shepherd's way to describe a sheep that is heavy with wool or one about to give birth who gets turned over on its back and cannot get up without help. Unless a shepherd finds such sheep, they will ultimately die. Therefore, a shepherd must sometimes renew or restore the life of his sheep.

Earlier in our study we considered the meaning of *Yahweh Rophe* (I am the One who heals). We all need the spiritual healing and restoration that only He can give. Apart from such a ministry of mercy, we surely would perish.

Verse 3b: "He leads me along the right paths for His name's sake." Frequent references occur in the Bible to God's people being led like sheep. One such passage is found in Jeremiah 23:1–8. Here Yahweh issues a warning to false shepherds who have led His people astray, scattering them among other nations. His promise is to raise up a "righteous Branch of David" who will be like a good shepherd gathering Israel and bringing them back to the right way. The name of this special person will be "The

LORD Our Righteousness" (Jer. 23:6). As we learned earlier, this name is *Yahweh Tsidkenu.*

The psalmist confessed his confidence that he would be led along the right paths by this special shepherd "for His name's sake." His name is *Our Righteousness,* and He will be true to that name by always leading His people in the right way—the way that is best for them.

Verse 4: "Even when I go through the darkest valley, I fear no danger, for You are with me: Your rod and Your staff—they comfort me." In order to reach the higher pastures in summertime, the shepherd led his sheep upward through dark passageways. Sheep were fearful of these unfamiliar, dangerous trails. The good shepherd always stayed near the sheep using his rod and staff as needed to protect his flock and bring them safely through. The sheep were comforted and delivered from fear by the faithful shepherd's presence.

The prophet Ezekiel was sent by God to give a series of messages to His people during the years of their captivity in Babylon. These displaced pilgrims often felt abandoned by God since they were far from Jerusalem and the Temple. However, the prophet's final word was one of hope; he ends his messages with the promise of a restored city. His final words are: "The name of the city from that day on will be Yahweh Is There" (Ezek. 48:35). This combination name is *Yahweh Shammah.*

Just as David affirmed his deliverance from fear because of the presence of Yahweh, we also may claim the same comfort. Listen to these words of promise: "Do not fear, for I am with you; do not be afraid, for I am your God. I will strengthen you; I will help you; I will hold on to you with my righteous right hand" (Isa. 41:10).

Verse 5: "You prepare a table before me in the presence of my enemies; You anoint my head with oil; my cup overflows." When the sheep have safely passed through the dark valleys and arrive at the upper pastures, they find the place prepared for them by the shepherd. All poisonous weeds and threatening predators have been removed; the banquet table of lush green grass is spread before them. In addition, the caring shepherd attends personally to each sheep, pouring soothing oil on each one's head, and offering a cup brimmed full of clean water.

These verses present a picture of triumph over enemies and the enjoyment of the fruit of victory. We must recall the name *Yahweh Nissi*—I AM the One who gives victory. Whatever may threaten the safety and security of His people is conquered by Him who overcame all challenges of the adversary, even the final enemy—death itself. Surely we are more than conquerors through Him who loved us.

Verse 6: "Only goodness and faithful love will pursue me all the days of my life, and I will dwell in the house of the LORD as long as I live." As the psalmist anticipates the future, he affirms his belief that throughout the long journey of life, two essential expressions of care will be provided—goodness and faithful love. He refers to the same goodness and faithful love that accompanied him in the past.

Finally, the image changes at the end of the journey from the sheep/shepherd motif to that of guest/host. The pilgrim has arrived in the house of the LORD. No longer does he need a shepherd; he is at home. Now the emphasis is on settling down and enjoying the eternal fellowship of the perfect Host.

This lovely poem of life begins and ends with *Yahweh*. How appropriate since He is Alpha and Omega, the first and the last, the beginning and the end. The Shepherd's Psalm is such a powerful statement of the meaning of His name—I AM whatever you need!

Psalm 23 and the Combination Names of Yahweh

The biblical number seven is often the number of completion. Here are seven names of Yahweh that reveal His complete provision for all our needs.

"The LORD is my shepherd."	Yahweh Rohi (I AM the Shepherd)
"There is nothing I lack."	Yahweh Yireh (I AM the Provider)
"He lets me lie down in green pastures; He leads me beside quiet waters."	Yahweh Shalom (I AM Peace)
"He renews my life."	Yahweh Rophe (I AM Healing)
"He leads me along the right paths for His name sake."	Yahweh Tsidkenu (I AM Righteousness)
"Even when I go through the darkest valley, I fear no danger, for You are with me: Your rod and Your staff—they comfort me."	Yahweh Shammah (I AM There)
"You prepare a table before me in the presence of my enemies; You anoint my head with oil; my cup overflows."	Yahweh Nissi (I AM Victory)

"Only goodness and faithful love will pursue me all the days of my life, and I will dwell in the house of the LORD as long as I live."

Study Guide

Standing at the Bush

- When you first discovered that the Lord is your shepherd, what came to your mind?
- How does Psalm 23 affirm your need for a personal relationship with God?

Seeing at the Bush

- Read Psalms 23:2. What provisions has Yahweh made so we can rest peacefully?
- List the seven combination names of Yahweh suggested by Psalm 23. Beside each name describe a personal need fulfilled by Yahweh.

Sharing from the Bush

- Tell a friend how the faithful Shepherd has comforted you and delivered you from fear.
- Write a paraphrase of Psalm 23 using your name rather than pronouns referring to David.

Chapter Twelve

Yahweh Sabaoth

(yah-WEH se-ba-OATH)

יהוה צבאות

One very interesting fact regarding these combination names is that they first appear in Scripture during a time of special need, a situation where divine provision intersects with human need. For example, the first occurrence of *Yahweh Sabaoth* is in 1 Samuel. This interesting book of Israel's history follows the period of the Judges (approximately 1380–1060 BC) when God's people experienced many cycles of highs and lows regarding their relationship with God.

Just prior to these 300 years of decline, Joshua led Israel to overcome most of the inhabitants of the Promised Land. Thus Israel was claiming her inheritance and enjoying the benefits of God's blessings. However, with the passing of Joshua, a spiritual decline began as the people turned from God to worship idols. Thus the long era of ups and downs set in. The book of Judges ends with this sad commentary on the condition of Israel: "In those days there was no king in Israel; everyone did whatever he wanted" (Judg. 21:25).

First Samuel begins the account of how God raised up a leader (Saul) who brought restoration and unity to His chosen people. I share this background information to set the stage for the first appearance of *Yahweh Sabaoth*. Chapter One of 1 Samuel begins with the story of Elkanah, a devout man who made an annual pilgrimage from his home to Shiloh, the center of worship where the tabernacle was located at that time. The text reads: "This man would go up from his town every year to worship and to sacrifice to the LORD of Hosts (*Yahweh Sabaoth*)" (1 Sam. 1:3).

Why is this significant combination-name of *Yahweh* recorded here for the first time in God's Word? We find the answer in the meaning of *Sabaoth*. As translated in the verse just cited, the term literally means "hosts." From other biblical references we learn that "hosts" includes all creation, such as angels, persons, stars and planets, plants and animals—everything. Elkanah and all the Israelites desperately needed a leader who would bring them together and bring back a sense of being God's chosen nation. Thus they looked beyond human resources to Yahweh who revealed Himself to them as *Yahweh Sabaoth*—the One who not only created all things but also rules over them.

Consider other biblical references to this sacred name. When young David engaged Goliath, the Philistine giant, he said to this ominous foe, "You come to me with a dagger, spear, and sword, but I come against you in the name of the LORD of hosts [*Yahweh Sabaoth*], the God of Israel's armies—you have defied Him. Today the LORD will hand you over to me ... then all the world will know that Israel has a God, and this whole assembly will know that it is not by sword or by spear that the LORD saves, for the battle is the LORD's. He will hand you over to us" (1 Sam. 17:45–47). David proceeded to slay this giant with a small stone propelled by his shepherd's sling.

God's people learned to appeal for help to the One who is the commander-in-chief of that army, inclusive of all the angels in heaven and on earth. How powerful is this host? We gain some insight into the awesomeness of the heavenly host from an incident recorded by the prophet Isaiah when God sent an angel against a huge Assyrian army. In one night this single angel killed 185,000 soldiers! (Read Isaiah

37:36.) Can you imagine the power residing in this host—power for the protection and deliverance of God's people?

Another expression of this divine creativeness is recorded in these words regarding our Savior: "For a child will be born for us, a son will be given to us, and the government will be on His shoulders. He will be named Wonderful Counselor, Mighty God, Eternal Father, Prince of Peace. The dominion will be vast, and its prosperity will never end. He will reign on the throne of David and over his kingdom, to establish and sustain it with justice and righteousness from now on and forever. The zeal of the LORD of Hosts [*Yahweh Sabaoth*] will accomplish this" (Isa. 9:6–7). An event of this magnitude only could be achieved by the ultimate sovereign ruler of this entire universe!

The final composition of the Old Testament is that of the prophet Malachi. In this brief document the term *Yahweh Sabaoth* occurs twenty-three times in four chapters! Notice the frequent references to God's "name" in this single verse, and what this name is: "'For My name will be great among the nations, from the rising of the sun to its setting. Incense and pure offerings will be presented in My name in every place because My name will be great among the nations,' says the LORD of Hosts [*Yahweh Sabaoth*]" (Mal. 1:11). This prophet was sent with a message of judgment due to the waywardness of God's people. However, the final word is one of hope: "So a book of remembrance was written before Him for those who feared Yahweh and had high regard for His name. 'They will be Mine,' says the LORD of Hosts [Yahweh Sabaoth], 'A special possession on the day I am preparing. I will have compassion on them as a man has compassion on his son who serves him'" (Mal. 3:16–17). God's final word before more than 400 years of silence (the time between Malachi and John the Baptist) was one of good news, and His final combination name is *Yahweh Sabaoth*.

We can understand why one writer states that the name *Yahweh Sabaoth* refers to "that heavenly aid available to God's people in their time of need." Here is God's name for man's extremity! And the most encouraging truth about Yahweh Sabaoth is His presence with us at all times. Listen to these inspiring words: "God is our refuge and strength, a helper who is always found in times of trouble. Therefore we will not be afraid, though the earth trembles and the mountains topple into the depths of the seas ... the LORD of Hosts [*Yahweh Sabaoth*] is with us; the God of Jacob is our stronghold" (Ps. 46:1–2, 7). What a blessed assurance! Why should we ever be fearful and anxious when such a source of unlimited power is our constant companion?

The words of Psalm 46 became the inspiration for Martin Luther as he composed the familiar hymn *A Mighty Fortress Is Our God* in 1529. Due to his reformed beliefs which were growing out of his study of the book of Romans, Luther experienced excommunication from the Roman Catholic Church, as well as numerous threats to his life. His classic expression of the assurance he found in Yahweh Sabaoth's presence and help is given in these words:

> A mighty fortress is our God, a bulwark never failing;
> Our helper He amid the flood of mortal ills prevailing.
> For still our ancient foe doth seek to work us woe—
> His craft and power are great, and, armed with cruel hate,
> On earth is not his equal.
>
> Did we in our own strength confide, our striving would be losing,
> Were not the right man on our side, the man of God's own choosing.
> Dost ask who that may be? Christ Jesus it is He—
> Lord Sabaoth His name, from age to age the same,
> And He must win the battle.

Like Martin Luther, we may claim those unlimited divine resources of deliverance and strength to help in times of our need.

One distinctive feature of Yahweh Sabaoth is the New Testament references to this name; two occurrences are cited. First, the apostle Paul quoted Isaiah 1:9 when he wrote, "If the Lord of Hosts [*Yahweh Sabaoth*] had not left us a seed, we would have become like Sodom, and we would have been made like Gomorrah" (Rom. 9:29). Then James warned unjust rich persons with these solemn words: "Look! The pay that you withheld from the workers who reaped your fields cries out, and the outcry of the harvesters has reached the ears of the Lord of Hosts [*Yahweh Sabaoth*]" (James 5:4). Both references appeal to the fact of Yahweh's supreme control over all creation.

Now consider a very significant addition to the name *Yahweh Sabaoth*. Unlike all the other such combination names, we find a third word added to this one. The first occurrence is found in 2 Samuel. David had succeeded Saul as king of all Israel and was able to capture the city of Jerusalem from the Jebusites. This interesting statement was recorded following his victory: "David became more and more powerful, and the LORD God of Hosts was with him" (2 Samuel 5:10). Notice these very meaningful words: "LORD God of Hosts." In the Hebrew language they are *Yahweh Elohim Sabaoth*.

We have just learned the amazing benefit communicated by *Yahweh Sabaoth*, now let's turn to *Elohim* [e-lo-HEEM]. The first mention of God in the Bible—"in the beginning God" (Gen. 1:1) introduces us to the term *Elohim*. The basic word for God is *El*; various meanings have been ascribed to this term, such as: absolute, unqualified, unlimited energy, power, mighty strength. *Elohim* is the plural form of *El*—not in the sense of more than one god, but rather the concept of the multifaceted nature of God. He is creator, judge, deliverer, redeemer, sovereign ruler, and much more. And some Bible interpreters find reasons to believe the triune nature of God, as Father, Son, and Holy Spirit, is found in *Elohim* as a plural word.

Elohim occurs more than 2,500 times in the Old Testament; sixteen of these are in the combination name *Yahweh Elohim Sabaoth*. Joining these three most power-filled words together produces a name that is beyond the ability of our finite minds to fully comprehend and appreciate. Notice again the context of that first occurrence—why did David become more and more powerful? "*Yahweh Elohim Sabaoth* was with him." David was not powerful in and of himself. When he approached the stronghold of the Jebusites in Jerusalem, they said to him, "You will never get in here. Even the blind and the lame can repel you" (2 Sam. 5:6). But he did overcome them, just like he overcame the giant, Goliath.

The secret of David's power and success was the fact that Yahweh Elohim Sabaoth was with him. Many others have discovered this same resource for overcoming various kinds of adversities and trials. The apostle Paul knew this secret and lived in the reality of it. Surely this fact is why he could make such a bold statement from his Roman imprisonment: "I am able to do all things through Him who strengthens me" (Phil. 4:13).

Is there some remote possibility that you and I could experience the same companionship with God, and could live a similar strong, victorious life as David, Paul, and countless others have? Absolutely! Remember His promise—"Do not fear, for I am with you; do not be afraid, for I am your God. I will strengthen you; I will help you; I will hold on to you with My righteous right hand" (Isa. 41:10).

Allow me to share a personal testimony at this point. Several years ago, as I studied these combination names, I was especially impressed by the name *Yahweh Elohim Sabaoth* and its power-filled significance. One day as I meditated on this unique combination of terms, I noticed that the first letters of these three words spell YES. I know that such an arrangement is not part of the inspiration of Scripture, or any kind of special revelation, but this simple acrostic has come to be very precious to me. Whenever I am facing some challenging situation—one that leaves me feeling very inadequate—I remember these three letters, and I confidently respond to the challenge: "YES, I can do this; YES, I can be all God calls me to be, because of the One who is with me, *Yahweh Elohim Sabaoth!*" I strongly recommend this acrostic for your consideration and practice.

Study Guide

Standing at the Bush

- Name some experiences of highs and lows regarding your relationship with God.
- What resources have you found helpful in these times?

Seeing at the Bush

- What does the name *Yahweh Sabaoth* mean to you?
- Why should a believer not be controlled by fear and anxiety?

Sharing from the Bush

- Inform a friend who is in a crisis how Yahweh Elohim Sabaoth can help.
- Explain to someone the meaning of the acrostic YES.

Chapter Thirteen

Yahweh Adonai

(yah-WEH a-do-NAI)

יהוה אדני

Adonai is the plural form of the Hebrew word *adon*, meaning "lord or ruler." *Adon* sometimes was used to refer to men who were husbands or a master of slaves, and implies a relationship of authority. *Adonai* occurs some 340 times in the Old Testament, is translated "Lord," and always refers to God.

The first occurrence of *adonai* is found in Genesis 15:2 where the word is used in combination with Yahweh: "But Abram said, 'Lord GOD, what can You give me, since I am childless and the heir of my house is Eliezer of Damascus?'" Notice the use of all capital letters for GOD. This actually is the Hebrew word *Yahweh* which most frequently is translated LORD (all capitals). However, in those references, such as Genesis 15:2, 8 where *adonai* and *Yahweh* occur together, translators use "Lord GOD" rather than "Lord LORD." Some confusion occurs in English translations by this use of upper and lower case. For example, in Genesis 2:4 the term "LORD God" is found. Following the practice of having *Yahweh* rendered as LORD, in upper case, and God, lower case, we know this is the Hebrew combination of *Yahweh Elohim*. Whereas "Lord GOD," as mentioned above, is *adonai Yahweh*.

The apparent reason for the frequent use of this interesting combination of *adonai Yahweh* is to give emphasis to Yahweh's sovereign control over all humankind. Consider this prayer of David: "Who am I, Lord GOD, and what is my house that You have brought me this far? What You have done so far was a little thing to You, Lord GOD, for You have also spoken about Your servant's house in the distant future. And this is a revelation for mankind, Lord GOD" (2 Sam. 7:18–19). This prayer continues through verse 29 and contains a total of eight uses of the term "Lord GOD" (*Yahweh Adonai*). David sought to acknowledge that every expression of God's favor to him and to all his descendents was a revelation of His sovereign control and favor.

One interesting statement where both LORD and Lord are used is found in Psalm 16:2 in these words of David: "I said to the LORD [*Yahweh*], 'You are my Lord [*adonai*]; I have no good beside you.'" And a similar expression occurs in Psalms 110:1, "The LORD declared to my Lord, 'Sit at My right hand until I make Your enemies Your footstool.'" Both of these examples show the use of the same English word, *Lord*, to translate two Hebrew words, *Yahweh* and *adonai*. As stated earlier, translators distinguish the difference by the use of upper and lower case letters.

The prophet Ezekiel used *Yahweh Adonai* more frequently than any other biblical writer. This combination is found more than 200 times in his book. The prophet sought to give authority and truthfulness to all his messages by declaring that the source of all he said was the Lord GOD. For example, in chapter 14, these two phrases: "This is what the Lord GOD says" and "The declaration of the Lord GOD" occur nine times. Ezekiel was determined to validate all his warnings and predictions by reminding his hearers that what he said came directly from the supreme ruler of the universe—the only One who could accomplish such promises.

The original Greek language of the New Testament has two words that are translated by the same English word "lord." These terms are *kurios*, meaning supreme in authority, and *despotes*, referring to an absolute ruler, such as a despot. Let's examine a few of these references that point out the supreme authority of Jesus. When the apostle Peter preached to a group of Gentiles in the house of Cornelius, he said, "He [God] sent the message to the sons of Israel, proclaiming the good news of peace through Jesus Christ—He is Lord of all" (Acts 10:36). Later, Paul wrote: "Therefore, whether we live or die, we belong to the Lord. Christ died and came to life for this: that He might rule over both the dead and the living" (Rom. 14:8–9), and this classic statement: "For this reason God also highly exalted Him and gave Him the name that is above every name, so that at the name of Jesus every knee should bow— of those who are in heaven and on earth and under the earth—and every tongue should confess that Jesus Christ is Lord, to the glory of God the Father" (Phil. 2:9–11).

Thus the Old Testament name *Yahweh Adonai* finds its fullest expression in the New Testament Messiah—the Lord Jesus Christ. He is the absolute and sovereign ruler over all His creation. The apostle John was given a vision in which he saw Jesus as a rider on a white horse. John reported: "on His robe and on His thigh He has a name written: KING OF KINGS AND LORD OF LORDS" (Rev. 19:16). One very significant result of His supremacy is the sobering fact that the day is coming when, as Paul wrote, "God also highly exalted Him and gave Him the name that is above every name, so that at the name of Jesus every knee should bow—of those who are in heaven and on earth and under the earth—and every tongue should confess that Jesus Christ is Lord, to the glory of God the Father" (Phil. 2:9–11).

Conclusion: We have examined a total of ten combination names of Yahweh; more can be found, but these are given in God's Word to help us in the following ways:

- That we may know more of who He is and what He wants to do for us.

- That we may claim by faith every benefit He provides.
- That we may worship Him in a more meaningful manner.
- That we may be better witnesses to others of who He is and what He will do.

Study Guide

Standing at the Bush

- What are some ways you have tried to be the lord of your own life?
- Relate what caused you to turn to Jesus as Lord.

Seeing at the Bush

- Why did Ezekiel so often remind his people that Yahweh Adonai is in control?
- What is your favorite biblical statement regarding the sovereignty of Jesus?

Sharing at the Bush

- Read Acts 10:36. How can you communicate the fact that Jesus is Lord of all?
- The next time you are with someone who is anxious and troubled, inform them of the meaning of Yahweh Adonai.

Part Three

New Testament Names

Chapter Fourteen
What about the Name of Jesus?

One very reasonable question is often raised at this point: Why do we not find references in the New Testament to these Old Testament names for God? In order to answer this question we must remember that the Bible is one book, comprised of two parts but with one message—God's revelation of Himself and His plan for all creation.

Throughout the first part (Old Testament), no visible revelation of God in human form is found. He revealed Himself by various names, titles, and word pictures. Thus we have the names, such as *Yahweh Rohi* ("I AM the Shepherd"), to help readers understand His nature, and *Yahweh Yireh* ("I AM the One who provides"), to express what He will do for His people. All these terms were the beginning of God's self-disclosure.

The second part of God's word (New Testament) opens with these instructive words: "The historical record of Jesus Christ, the Son of David, the Son of Abraham" (Matt. 1:1). This statement reaches back more than 400 years to the Old Testament record and connects those events and names with all that is introduced by the birth of Jesus. John's way of stating this fact is found in this form: "In the beginning was the Word, and the Word was with God, and the Word was God ... the Word became flesh and took up residence among us. We observed His glory, the glory as the One and Only Son from the Father.... No one has

79

ever seen God, The One and Only Son—the One who is at the Father's side—He has revealed Him" (John 1:1–2, 14, 18).

The most profound statement of Jesus regarding His disclosure of God occurs in this response to a request by Philip: "'Lord,' said Philip, 'show us the Father, and that's enough for us.' Jesus said to him, 'Have I been among you all this time without your knowing Me, Philip? The one who has seen Me has seen the Father. How can you say, "Show us the Father"? Don't you believe that I am in the Father and the Father is in Me? The words I speak to you I do not speak on My own. The Father who lives in Me does His works. Believe Me that I am in the Father and the Father is in Me. Otherwise believe because of the works themselves'" (John 14:8–11).

Jesus came to earth to be the personal, visible, human revelation of Yahweh. One very significant piece of evidence of this truth is found in the Father's choice of a name for His Son. Before Jesus was born, Joseph was given a dream in which an angel said to him, "Joseph, son of David, don't be afraid to take Mary as your wife, because what has been conceived in her is by the Holy Spirit. She will give birth to a son, and you are to name Him Jesus, because He will save His people from their sins" (Matt. 1:20–21). Why did the Father choose this particular name? Look at the meaning of this word. The name Jesus comes from the Hebrew word for Joshua (*Yeshua*), which means "Yahweh saves." (See the footnote on this verse in the *Holman Christian Standard Bible*.)

The name Jesus (*Yeshua*) occurs over 700 times in the New Testament. Each of these speaks to us of His relationship with Yahweh. And every mention of Jesus reminds us of God's new and improved revelation of Himself in terms of a visible, human person. All those Old Testament combination names of God find their fulfillment in Jesus. In other words, Jesus Christ is the embodiment of *Yireh* (provider), *Rophi* (healer), *Nissi* (overcomer), *M'kaddesh* (sanctifier), *Shalom* (peacemaker), *Tsidkenu* (justifier), *Shammah* (companion), *Rohi* (caregiver), *Sabaoth* (supreme ruler), *Adonai* (sovereign Lord), and much more! As Paul wrote to the Colossians, "He [Jesus Christ] is the image of the invisible God … . For in Him the entire fullness of God's nature dwells bodily, and you have been filled by Him, who is the head over every ruler and authority" (Col 1:15; 2:9–10).

We must add a comment on the word "Christ." The name Jesus was rather common in New Testament days. However, no one other than Jesus of Nazareth, the son of Mary, was known as Jesus Christ, or Jesus the Christ. *Christ* is the Greek form of the Hebrew word translated *Messiah,* meaning "anointed one." *Jesus* is the personal name of our Lord; *Christ* is His official title. The first announcement of this truth is found in Andrew's words to his brother Simon: "We have found the Messiah! [which means *Anointed One*], and he brought Simon to Jesus" (John 1:41–42). The term *Christ* (Messiah) designates that person who became the fulfillment of all the Old Testament predictions regarding God's promise to send a person who would be everything His people need—a Savior, Redeemer, King, Shepherd, and Lord.

Study Guide

The Study Guides for Part Three are arranged in the following acrostic (BUSH) outline:

B—(Basic truth about Jesus) Jesus came to earth to be the personal, visible, human revelation of Yahweh. How is this truth related to the birth of Jesus?

U—(Using this information about Jesus) His birth opened a new understanding of who Jesus is. When was the first time you recognized the significance of the birth of Jesus?

S—(Searching for more truth about Jesus) Locate the name "Jesus" in a Bible concordance; discover three occasions when His name made a difference to someone.

H—(Honoring the truth about Jesus through prayer) Offer a prayer using the name "Yeshua," expressing gratitude for all this name means.

Now join me in an interesting and most helpful study of a series of claims Jesus made about Himself—claims that connect Him directly to Yahweh.

Chapter Fifteen
Jesus as the I AM

You will recall our earlier consideration of God's self-revelation to Moses at the burning bush (see Chapter 1). The word *YHWH*, meaning, "I AM WHO I AM," was a clear disclosure of the most basic truth about God. Since Jesus came to be the visible, human expression of God, we should not be surprised that He often referred to Himself by the words "I AM."

A series of these statements is found only in the Gospel of John. In fact, Jesus used the words "I am" twenty-three times. The first occurrence we will consider is when He initiated a conversation with a woman who came to draw water from a well in Samaria. She said, "I know that Messiah is coming (who is called Christ). When He comes, He will explain everything to us." (John 4:25). Jesus made a simple, yet bold, announcement to her: "I am [He], the One speaking to you." You will notice how the translators put brackets around "He," in order to give a better reading. However, in the original Greek text, His response was given in two words, meaning "I am."

John chapter 8 records three more of these "I am" statements. The first was spoken by Jesus in response to His enemies who refused to accept His claim to be sent from God. He boldly said to them, "If you do not believe that I am [He], you will die in your sins" (John 8:24). Again,

Jesus's actual words were "If you do not believe that I am, you will die in your sins."

The next "I am" occurred later in the same conversation. They asked, "Who are You?" Jesus answered by saying, "When you lift up the Son of Man, then you will know that I am [He], and that I do nothing on My own ..." (John 8:28). He was referring to His being lifted up on the cross—"then you will know that I am."

As this lengthy dialog continued, the Pharisees brought up the subject of Abraham and asked, "Are You greater than our father Abraham who died? Who do You pretend to be?" Jesus replied with this amazing claim, "Your father Abraham was overjoyed that he would see My day; he saw it and rejoiced." To this the Jews replied, "You aren't 50 years old yet, and You've seen Abraham?" Jesus said, "I assure you: Before Abraham was, I am" (John 8:58). What an astounding, incredible claim! Jesus knew that such words would jeopardize His life. Sure enough, the Jews immediately picked up stones to kill Him, but He quickly escaped.

This last claim is especially impressive because Jesus thereby identified Himself in His pre-incarnate condition. Here was a man who said He existed 2,100 years earlier, long before Abraham. What a clear claim to be both human and divine! And what a strong affirmation of His identity with Yahweh, the One revealed to Moses at the burning bush. Jesus (Yeshua) identified Himself with God. As He later said to these same enemies, "The Father and I are one" (John 10:30).

Now focus on one other situation where our Lord made this astounding claim. When the soldiers came to arrest Him, He asked them who they were searching for. They replied, "Jesus the Nazarene." The text records His response three times; three times He said to them, "I am" (John 18:5, 6, 8). Have you wondered why these strong, armed soldiers "stepped back and fell to the ground" when Jesus said, "I am"? I believe they were overpowered by the reality that they were in the presence of the eternal, omnipotent God—the I AM of the burning bush! There was an overwhelming, invisible force that literally forced these rugged warriors to fall back on the ground. Jesus could easily have spoken one word and completely destroyed every one of those soldiers. However, He knew they were a part of God's eternal plan, so He submitted Himself to be arrested by them.

Next, I want to guide us through a series of seven I AM claims Jesus made, using various metaphors found in the Gospel of John. Let's preface this study by observing that Jesus is recognized as the most effective of all great teachers. One reason for this reputation is His ability to teach hearers about spiritual truths they did not understand by comparing these mysteries to physical things they did understand. Many of these I AM statements reveal this truth, such as I AM: Bread, light, a door, a shepherd, a vine. By using these metaphors, Jesus revealed the truth about things unseen through comparisons with things seen.

Join me in a survey of these significant statements. Notice how each of these relates to His saving relationship to us; remember that His name *Yeshua* means "Yahweh is salvation." This mission to provide salvation is most clearly revealed by His experience with a rich tax collector named Zaccheus. Jesus invited Himself to be a guest in this man's home. During that brief encounter, Zaccheus was delivered from his greed as well as from the guilt of all his many sins. Jesus joyfully proclaimed, "Today salvation has come to this house, because he too is a son of Abraham. For the Son of Man has come to seek and to save the lost" (Luke 19:9–10). When He said, "Salvation has come to this house," He referred to Himself—Yeshua is salvation.

Study Guide

B—(Basic truth about Jesus) Jesus often referred to Himself by the words I AM. Locate the Scripture reference where Yahweh first revealed Himself to Moses with these words.

U—(Using the truth about Jesus) What three claims did Jesus make about Himself to verify the fact that He is the I AM?

S—(Searching for more truth about Jesus) Jesus referred to Himself as I AM more than twenty times in the Gospel of John. Use a Bible concordance to discover five references to these I AM statements that are not listed in this chapter.

H—(Honoring the truth about Jesus through prayer) Thank Jesus for revealing Himself as the I AM; ask Him to make this truth more meaningful to you.

Chapter Sixteen
I Am the Bread of Life

The statement "I am the bread of life" is found in the sixth chapter of the Gospel of John, a passage beginning with the only miracle of Jesus recorded in all four gospels—the feeding of the 5,000. On the day following this sign miracle, many of those who were fed crossed the Sea of Galilee and came to Capernaum, seeking Jesus. When they found Him, He spoke rather bluntly and said, "I assure you: You are looking for Me, not because you saw the signs, but because you ate the loaves and were filled. Don't work for the food that perishes but for the food that lasts for eternal life, which the Son of Man will give you, because God the Father has set His seal of approval on Him" (John 6:26–27).

You will notice that the subject of what follows is "the food that lasts for eternal life." Jesus continued His message to these seekers by saying, "My Father gives you the real bread from heaven. For the bread of God is the One who comes down from heaven and gives life to the world." Then He made this bold claim: "I am the bread of life. No one who comes to Me will ever be hungry, and no one who believes in Me will ever be thirsty again" (John 6:35).

He is, of course, referring to spiritual hunger and thirst. Jesus used this analogy to teach important truths about His willingness to meet His hearer's greatest needs. Eleven times in this chapter He refers to Himself as "bread." What can we learn from this word picture? First,

Jesus offers us that which is essential. Food is not a luxury; we must have it, or we die. In a similar way, every person is spiritually dead apart from Jesus—the bread of life.

Jesus did not come simply to improve human life, to make our lives better; He came to give life to the dead. Later in this same chapter, Jesus spoke these strange-sounding words: "I assure you: Unless you eat the flesh of the Son of Man and drink His blood, you do not have life in yourselves" (John 6:53). Then He explained that His words were not to be taken literally but spiritually: "The Spirit is the One who gives life. The flesh doesn't help at all. The words that I have spoken to you are spirit and are life" (John 6:63).

This verse leads to a second truth: We must partake of the Bread of Life. Jesus used the term "eat" seven times in this passage. A person who is starving for food could die with bread in his hand if he never ate it. In a similar manner, those who know of Jesus must receive Him by faith in order to have eternal life. This fact is the truth Jesus sought to affirm by calling for hearers to eat His flesh and drink His blood—we must partake of Him spiritually.

One further encouraging truth is communicated by these words previously quoted: "No one who comes to Me will ever be hungry, and no one who believes in Me will ever be thirsty again." Jesus satisfies! He meets every spiritual need completely and forever. A person who is in close fellowship with Jesus can never truthfully claim that something is missing from his or her life. The spiritual nourishment Jesus gives lasts forever. As Paul wrote from his imprisonment in Rome: "In any and all circumstances I have learned the secret of being content—whether well-fed or hungry, whether in abundance or in need. I am able to do all things through Him who strengthens me" (Phil. 4:12–13).

Josiah Conder (1789–1855) was an English author and publisher. He composed many hymn texts; one of these is a Communion song that speaks of Jesus as the bread of life.

Bread of Heaven on Thee We Feed

Bread of Heaven on Thee we feed,
For thy flesh is meat indeed.
Ever let our souls be fed
With this true and living bread.
Day by day, with strength supplied
Thro' the life of Him who died,

Vine of Heaven, Thy blood supplies
This blest cup of sacrifice;
Lord, Thy wounds our healing give,
To Thy cross we look and live:
Jesus, may we ever be
Grafted, rooted, built in Thee.

Allow me to share a personal testimony at this point. Each morning I begin the day with a private reminder of who Jesus is and what my relationship to Him must be. I do this by eating a small piece of bread while prayerfully quoting the first stanza of Conder's hymn. Then I drink my cup of coffee as I pray the second stanza. This simple spiritual discipline has made a great difference in my fellowship with the bread of life!

Study Guide

B—(Basic truth about Jesus) All our spiritual needs are satisfied when we receive Jesus.

U—(Using the truth about Jesus) Name some ways you can feed on the Bread of Life. How are you practicing these opportunities?

S—(Searching for more truth about Jesus) Explore John 6:22–59, making a list of further information regarding Jesus as the bread of life. Write a personal statement describing what Jesus means to you as the bread of your life.

H—(Honoring the truth about Jesus through prayer) As you pray daily, include thanks to Jesus for being the complete satisfaction for all your spiritual needs.

Chapter Seventeen
I Am the Light of the World

The Gospel of John, chapter 8 begins with the account of the Pharisees bringing to Jesus a woman who they say was "caught in adultery." Obviously, these religious critics were seeking to challenge the credibility of Jesus. If He agreed that she should be stoned to death, as ordered by the Law (Deut. 22:22–24), they would accuse Him of not being compassionate and not "the friend of sinners." On the other hand, if He released her, He would be charged with not upholding the divine Law. John comments: "They asked this to trap Him, in order that they might have evidence to accuse Him" (John 8:6).

You may recall that Jesus wisely responded by saying, "The one without sin among you should be the first to throw a stone at her." Rather than judge the woman, He judged the judges!

Jesus's next words to these self-righteous enemies were in the form of His second I AM claim: "I am the light of the world. Anyone who follows Me will never walk in the darkness but will have the light of life" (John 8:12). Light and darkness in Scripture represent truth and error, good and evil. His immediate application of these words was to those religious leaders who were blind to truth; they were in moral and spiritual darkness.

Many other teachers have expressed truth in their words, but none of them could accurately assert that they, in themselves, were *the truth*.

Jesus boldly announced that the light of truth He came to reveal was expressed by His life! In other words, He came to give light by "the light of life"—His life.

Consider various areas where Jesus revealed truth. First, His life reveals the truth about God. As mentioned earlier in our study, He said, "The one who has seen Me has seen the Father." Jesus literally turned on the light that revealed who God is and what He does. Second, His life shows the truth about humankind. Because Jesus was human, as well as divine, we see in His life what we can and should be—we see both our shortcomings and our potential.

Furthermore, Jesus exposes the truth about this world—a system of values and practices that are controlled by Satan, contrary to God. We live in a world that totally rejects God's love and truth, as seen in Jesus.

Many other aspects of life could be cited that were illumined by the life of Christ. One other is especially significant: because of Jesus, we know the truth about death and what lies beyond the grave. (More about this subject will be covered in His claim as the resurrection and the life.)

Just think of how ignorant we would be in every one of these important subjects apart from Jesus. His promise becomes so very encouraging as He says, "Anyone who follows Me will never walk in the darkness but will have the light of life." To follow Him means to trust Him so completely that we commit ourselves to live in fellowship with Him through obedience to His commands.

We must add one more reminder at this point. Jesus, the Light of the World, declared that all who choose to follow Him would not only have the light of His life, but would therefore become lights in the world themselves! Recall His words from the Sermon on the Mount: "You are the light of the world. A city situated on a hill cannot be hidden. No one lights a lamp and puts it under a basket, but rather on a lamp-stand, and it gives light for all who are in the house. In the same way, let your light shine before men, so that they may see your good works and give glory to your Father in heaven" (Matt. 5:14–16).

I have sometimes illustrated this truth by holding up a light bulb and saying, "Believers are like light bulbs; we have no power of our own, but when we are connected to Jesus, the light of His life shines through us!" Our responsibility is not to *make* the light shine; rather, as He said, to *let* the light shine. Two challenges are presented here: First, the challenge of staying firmly connected to Him—abiding in Him through prayer. Second, being diligent to make sure His light can shine clearly through us. This means to avoid whatever hinders that light. When we fail to do this, we must confess sins and claim this promise: "If we confess our sins, He is faithful and righteous to forgive us our sins and to cleanse us from all unrighteousness" (1 John 1:9).

Study Guide

B—(Basic truth about Jesus) Jesus came to reveal all we need to know about God.

U—(Using the truth about Jesus) Our spiritual darkness is overcome when we receive Jesus as the Light of our world. What evidence of this darkness can you see in others, and how can you help them?

S—(Searching for more truth about Jesus) Read the following references and from these write a summary of what they mean: Psalm 27:1; John 3:19, 9:5, 12:35–36; Eph. 5:8; 1 John 1:5.

H—(Honoring the truth about Jesus through prayer) Read Matthew 5:14–16. Offer a prayer based on these words.

Chapter Eighteen

I Am the Door

Jesus lived in an agricultural environment. His hearers were all well acquainted with planting seed, growing and harvesting grain, tending livestock, and everything related to farming and cattle raising. Thus many of Jesus's teachings make reference to these familiar experiences.

When He said, "I am the door of the sheep" (John 10:7), His audience understood what He meant far better than we. The term "door of the sheep" comes from the following description: During the day, shepherds led their flocks to various pastures for grazing. In the evening, they looked for a place of shelter and safety. Sometimes a large, open enclosure surrounded by a low stone wall was available. Here shepherds would leave their sheep for the night, along with the flocks of other shepherds. The entrance would be a narrow opening and quite often the shepherd or some hired attendant (doorkeeper) would lie down and sleep across the opening to prevent the sheep or anything else from passing through. This person became "the door" of the sheepfold.

Jesus is "the door" in the sense of being the way of entering the kingdom of God. Notice the contrast between Him and the Pharisees. The ninth chapter of John tells the story of a man who was blind from birth and was healed by Jesus. After the Pharisees questioned this man, they cast him out of their synagogue. The blind man believed Jesus was sent by God to perform such miracles. The Pharisees closed the door to this beggar while Jesus opened the door, welcoming him to an abundant life.

His words to these false teachers were, "I am the door. If anyone enters by Me, he will be saved and will come in and go out and find pasture. A thief comes only to steal and to kill and to destroy. I have come that they may have life and have it in abundance" (John 10:9–10). The Pharisees believed and taught that the way of entering God's kingdom was first to be born a Jew, then to keep God's laws as they interpreted them. Apart from having the right parents and conforming to the right rituals and works, a person had no hope of belonging to their "flock."

Jesus contradicted these teachings of the Pharisees. He described the way of entering the kingdom to be through trusting Him—an entrance by faith, not works. Moreover, He included all non-Jews (Gentiles) when He said, "I have other sheep that are not of this fold; I must bring them also, and they will listen to My voice. Then there will be one flock, one shepherd" (John 10:16). What good news! How easy for us to understand and to accept this truth.

As the door, Jesus not only provides us with an entrance into God's kingdom, but also protection from Satan, our spiritual enemy. In the passage quoted above, Jesus speaks of the thief that "comes only to steal and to kill and to destroy." These words describe Satan's plan for every person—to steal them from God, kill their usefulness to Him, and destroy them forever in Hell. But the door prevents this; He keeps the thief outside. Listen to these comforting words from the psalmist:

> The LORD will protect you from all harm;
> He will protect your life.
> The LORD will protect your coming and going
> both now and forever. (Ps. 121:7–8)

Now consider the meaning of what Jesus (the door) said about "life in abundance." In the original language of the New Testament the word *abundance* means "an exceeding measure, more than the ordinary." Jesus is the "door" to an entirely new life, one that abounds in every way. In this passage He alludes to this exceeding measure by His promise to those who place their trust in Him: "He will be saved and will come in and go out and find pasture" (John 10: 9). Everything that a sheep might need or want is provided—in abundance—by Jesus, the door.

We who have discovered the door and entered the kingdom by trusting Him now have the responsibility and privilege of helping others pass through the same entrance. An old verse states:

> Have you had a kindness shown? Pass it on.
> 'Twas not meant for you alone. Pass it on.
> Let it travel down the years.
> Let it dry another's tears.
> 'Til in heaven the deed appears. Pass it on.

May we be faithful to pass on to others the truth about Jesus, the door.

The next I AM is found in this same context, continuing the same metaphor of sheep and shepherds.

Study Guide

B—(Basic truth about Jesus) Jesus is the entrance to the Kingdom of God.

U—(Using the truth about Jesus) How many doors are there to the abundant life? Who led you to the door and when did you enter?

S—(Searching for more truth about Jesus) Jesus is the door to an entirely new life. Using other biblical references, describe this life.

H—(Honoring the truth about Jesus through prayer) Thank Jesus (the door) for opening the way to the abundant provision for all you need.

Chapter Nineteen
I Am the Good Shepherd

Humans often are compared to animals by sayings such as: "He is as strong as an ox," or "she is as stubborn as a mule," or "he eats like a horse," or "she sings like a bird." The favorite biblical comparison of humankind to an animal is that of sheep. For example, the psalmist declared, "We are ... the sheep of His pasture" (Ps. 100:3). Such a metaphor is not very complimentary because sheep are among the least intelligent and most dependent creatures on earth.

Jesus chose this word picture to communicate what we are and what He came to do for us when He declared, "I am the good shepherd" (John 10:11). First, we are all like sheep in the sense that we are prone to go astray from God. As Isaiah wrote, "We all went astray like sheep; we all have turned to our own way" (Isa. 53:6). Just as sheep, when left to themselves, will wander off from the flock, so we all choose our way rather than God's way. This kind of waywardness is what the Bible describes as sin.

Moreover, we also are like sheep because of their dependent nature. They are not capable of defending themselves against enemies such as wolves. And if they become "cast down," they will die unless someone helps them. (See the description of this on page 59.)

Sheep must have a good shepherd—someone to guide them, protect them, and care for them—or else they will perish. The same is true of us;

we need a good caregiver, and Jesus came to be all we need. Notice how He expresses this truth: "The good shepherd lays down his life for the sheep" (John 10:11). What a supreme sacrifice He was willing to make for us! On another occasion He spoke of this same matter when He said, "No one has greater love than this, that someone would lay down his life for his friends. You are My friends if you do what I command you" (John 15:13–14).

The result of His sacrifice upon the cross is the gift of eternal life. Apart from Jesus, we are spiritually dead in our sins. We are certain to perish eternally. However, His death makes possible an eternal life. Later in this chapter Jesus said of His sheep, "My sheep hear My voice, I know them, and they follow Me. I give them eternal life, and they will never perish—ever!" (John 10:27–28). A strong emphasis on eternal security is found in the grammatical structure of this statement. In the original Greek language of this verse, a double negative is used for emphasis. A literal rendering would be, "I give them eternal life, and they will *not never* perish." Notice how the HCSB translation expresses this: "They will never perish—ever!"

Further assurance of eternal security is found as Jesus went on to say, "No one will snatch them out of My hand. My Father who has given them to Me, is greater than all. No one is able to snatch them out of the Father's hand. The Father and I are one" (John 10:28–30). The Good Shepherd promises to protect and care for His sheep eternally. What complete assurance and security all believers have in Him!

The fact of our eternal security in Jesus is especially meaningful to me because I grew up in a denomination that taught otherwise. "Once saved, always saved" was a new concept to me when I first attended a Baptist church. I had been led to believe that after I received Jesus, I could choose to go away from Him, thus becoming lost again. Various "proof texts" were given to support this view. As a result, I lacked a sense of assurance of salvation because I knew I had sinned since being saved.

I remember a preacher illustrating eternal security by quoting the verses just mentioned from John 10:27–30. He put a coin in his hand

and closed it, saying, "We are like this coin in the hand of Jesus, who said, 'I give my sheep eternal life and no one can take them out of My hand.' We are secure because He holds us. Not only that, but we have double security, for Jesus said, 'My Father, who has given them to Me, is greater than all. No one is able to snatch them out of the Father's hand. The Father and I are one.'" The preacher put his other hand around the hand with the coin, saying, "See how both Jesus and the Father are keeping us safe and secure?"

That illustration is certainly not perfect, for we are not inanimate objects like coins; however, being kept eternally secure in the hands of Jesus and the Father is true. When Jesus said, "No one will snatch them out of My hand," He was referring to Satan. The devil is the only one who wants to take us away from Jesus, and he can't do it! The Good Shepherd pledges the permanent safety of all His sheep. (These words from John 10 remind us of our previous study of *Yahweh Rohi*. See pages 57–62.)

Remember that Jesus qualified His promises as the Good Shepherd by telling His hearers: "My sheep … follow Me" (John 10: 27). Simply claiming that we believe in Him is not enough; we must be serious about following Him, which means we must keep His commands. Just as there are false shepherds, there also are false sheep—those who say they are followers of Jesus, but do not maintain a lifestyle of obedience to Him.

Study Guide

B—(Basic truth about Jesus) Jesus, the Good Shepherd, laid down His life in order to provide eternal life for us and to protect us from our enemies.

U—(Using the truth about Jesus) How do you respond when you are tempted to doubt your salvation?

S—(Searching for more truth about Jesus) Why is claiming to believe in Jesus not enough? Read 1 John 5:11–13 to help with your answer.

H—(Honoring the truth about Jesus through prayer) Make Psalm 23 your personal prayer.

Chapter Twenty

I Am the Resurrection and the Life

As a pastor I have conducted many funerals. When the person who passed is a Christian, I often seek to comfort the family by referring to Jesus's words found in John 11:25–26, "I am the resurrection and the life. The one who believes in Me, even if he dies, will live. Everyone who lives and believes in Me will never die—ever." (In Chapter Nineteen we observed a similar emphasis using this strong double negative in John 10:28.)

If you read the first portion of John 11, you will understand the context in which these comforting words first were spoken. Jesus had three special friends who lived in the village of Bethany near Jerusalem: Mary, her sister Martha, and their brother Lazarus. When Jesus heard that Lazarus died, He deliberately delayed His visit to Mary and Martha until Lazarus had been in the tomb for four days. Upon His arrival, Martha went to meet Him, saying, "Lord, if You had been here, my brother wouldn't have died. Yet even now I know that whatever You ask from God, God will give you" (John 11:21–22).

Jesus replied, "Your brother will rise again." Martha assumed Jesus was referring to "the resurrection at the last day." But Jesus made the startling promise that He, Himself, was the Resurrection and the Life (quoted above). After Jesus proceeded to greet Mary, He asked where Lazarus was buried. As He stood before the large stone, covering the entrance to the cave, Jesus asked that the stone be removed. He then offered a prayer of thanks to the Father and with a loud voice called, "Lazarus, come out!" (One interpreter said, "If Jesus had not called Lazarus by name, He would have emptied every grave on earth!")

To the amazement of everyone, "The dead man came out bound hand and foot with linen strips and with his face wrapped in a cloth. Jesus said to the people standing by, 'Loose him and let him go'" (John 11:44). This miracle must have been most impressive to these witnesses. They recognized that only God could restore life to someone who had died and been in a tomb that long.

This event was a sign miracle in the sense of being a supernatural action that pointed beyond itself to a significant truth. Jesus was revealing the truth that He did not come merely to give life but to give Himself *as life*. He came not merely to give a resurrection to dead persons but to prove *He is resurrection*. In other words, Jesus offers Himself to meet these critical needs.

Death is the most certain and formidable enemy of humankind. The writer of Ecclesiastes observed, "There is … a time to give birth and a time to die" (Eccl. 3:1). Paul declared, "The last enemy to be abolished is death" (1 Cor. 15:26). Every person faces the inevitable reality of physical death; there is no escape. The good news of the gospel message provides hope as individuals face the reality of death.

Jesus came to offer more than an improved manner of life—more than health, wealth, and prosperity. He came to provide a new kind of life—eternal life. Quoting the apostle Paul again, "If we have placed our hope in Christ for this life only, we should be pitied more than anyone. But now Christ has been raised from the dead, the firstfruits of those who have fallen asleep. For since death came through a man, the resurrection of the dead also comes through a man. For just as in Adam all die, so also in Christ all will be made alive" (1 Cor. 15:19–22).

The original New Testament word for "resurrection" literally means "to cause to stand up." By identifying Himself as "the resurrection," Jesus promised victory over both spiritual and physical death. Believers are resurrected spiritually the moment they place their trust in Him for salvation. Their dead spirits are made alive, born again, and made to stand up. Moreover, even our physical bodies will eventually be resurrected. Our new bodies will be far superior to these "houses of clay" we now inhabit.

Consider one more quote from the most extensive Bible passage on the subject of the resurrection: "There are heavenly bodies and earthly bodies, but the splendor of the heavenly bodies is different from that of the earthly ones. There is a splendor of the sun, another of the moon, and another of the stars; for star differs from star in splendor. So it is with the resurrection of the dead: Sown in corruption, raised in incorruption; sown in dishonor, raised in glory; sown in weakness, raised in power; sown a natural body, raised a spiritual body" (1 Cor. 15:40–44).

Allow me to include another aspect of Jesus's work as the Resurrection and the Life.

We are told by John, regarding Jesus, "All things were created through Him, and apart from Him not one thing was created that has been created" (John 1:3). The earth and all life—plants, animals, humans—all are His creation. Originally this creation was perfect (Gen. 1–2). Then came sin and the subsequent curse on all creation (Gen. 3:14–19).

God's plan includes the eventual restoration of all creation—back to its original perfection. The prophet Isaiah was given these words from the Lord: "For I will create a new heaven and a new earth" (Isa. 65:17). Then the apostle Peter referred to a restored creation when he wrote: "But the Day of the Lord will come like a thief; on that day the heavens will pass away ... the elements will burn and be dissolved, and the earth and the works on it will be disclosed ... . But based on His promise, we wait for new heavens and a new earth, where righteousness will dwell" (2 Peter 3:10, 13). Finally, these words of the apostle John: "Then I saw a new heaven and a new earth, for the first heaven and the first earth had passed away" (Rev. 21:1).

These inspired statements point to a new creation of both the heavens and the earth—a new creation where sin and its consequences no longer exist. Who will accomplish this amazing miracle? John heard these words from Jesus seated on a throne in heaven, "Look! I am making everything new … I am the Alpha and the Omega, the Beginning and the End" (Rev. 21:5–6). The One who also is the Resurrection and the Life will literally resurrect the old sin-cursed heavens and earth, making them new and perfect. Just as believers will have a new resurrected body, they will live on a new resurrected earth.

All these wonders and mysteries are made possible by the resurrection of our Lord Jesus and His subsequent offer of Himself as our resurrection. Here is another amazing aspect of how the I AM meets every need in this life and beyond.

Study Guide

B—(Basic truth about Jesus) Jesus came to give Himself as the One who overcomes death for all who believe in Him.

U—(Using the truth about Jesus) Suppose medical tests revealed that you have a fatal disease—how would you respond?

S—(Searching for more truth about Jesus) Read the following: John 5:25–29; John 6:39–54; Romans 8:23; 1 Cor. 15:19–26. What hope for your future is revealed in these verses?

H—(Honoring the truth about Jesus through prayer) Express your gratitude to God for Jesus as your Resurrection and Life.

Chapter Twenty-One

I Am the Way, the Truth, and the Life

Jesus combined three of His previous claims in making this one: "I am the way [door of the sheep], the truth [light of the world], and the life [Resurrection and the Life]." In order to appreciate His repetition of these terms, we must examine the biblical background of each statement. The same is true of each I AM claim. They all relate to the context in which they occur.

Let's consider the setting for this statement. The apostle John is the only one who records most of the information in John 13—17. All these meaningful words and actions followed the final Passover meal. During that time of fellowship, Jesus shared disturbing news with the Twelve. First, He told them that one of them would betray Him (13:21–26), next He said He would soon be leaving them (13:33–36), and finally He foretold Peter's denial of Him (13:38). These facts greatly troubled the disciples.

Jesus sought to comfort Peter and these other chosen men by saying, "Your heart must not be troubled. Believe in God; believe also in Me. In My Father's house are many dwelling places; if not, I would have told you. I am going away to prepare a place for you. If I go away and prepare a place for you, I will come back and receive you to Myself, so that where

I am you may be also. You know the way where I am going" (John 14:1–4).

Thomas spoke for all the rest when he said, "Lord, we don't know where You're going. How can we know the way?" In response to this question, Jesus told him, "I am the way, the truth, and the life. No one comes to the Father except through Me" (John 14:6).

From this context, we understand what Jesus meant when He said, "I am the way." He answered Thomas's question: "How can we know the way?" Notice Jesus did not say, "I know the way," or "I will show you the way,"—rather, "I am the way." He is the way to the Father, and to the Father's house (heaven). Moreover, Jesus was very clear about being the *only* way—"No one comes to the Father except through Me." The way is inclusive in the sense of "whosoever will may come," but exclusive in the sense of being the one and only way. Our response should be one of gratitude that God, in His mercy and by His grace, has provided a way for all sinners to be reconciled and fully restored to Him forever. In addition, He offers a way for us to join Him in those specially prepared "dwelling places" in the Father's house.

Jesus also is the truth—the truth about God, this world, and humankind. Ultimate truth and reality finds its source in Jesus. As stated earlier, Jesus said, "I was born for this, and I have come into the world for this: to testify to the truth. Everyone who is of the truth listens to My voice" (John 18:37). Again, notice His words in this I AM claim—not "I know the truth," nor "I speak the truth," but "I am the truth." When we receive Jesus, we have the truth. What a wonder!

Finally, He is the life—the very life of God, eternal life, victorious life, abundant life, the life everyone desires to experience. Here is the uniqueness of the Christian message. Other religious leaders have promised a better life to those who choose to follow their teachings. But Jesus promises not a better life, but a new life—His life. As has been well stated, authentic Christianity is not our life made over; it is His life taking over! Eternal life is not our present life extended forever; eternal life is His life imparted to us forever. The apostle John expressed this truth in these terms: "God has given to us eternal life, and this life is in His Son. The one who has the Son has life. The one who doesn't have the Son of God does not have life" (1 John 5:11–12).

Before leaving this subject, I want to return to the fact of Jesus being the only way to God. Recent surveys have revealed that three-fourths of those who attend American Protestant churches believe there are many roads to God and eternal life. Among evangelical churches the number is lower (37%). Those of us who accept the Bible as being the inspired, reliable word of God must take Jesus's claim seriously. He is the ultimate authority in all matters of our faith and relationship to God. And Jesus said, "No one comes to the Father except through Me" (John 14:6).

I would like to believe that the majority of the people of this world will one day be in heaven. What did Jesus say about this? "Enter the narrow gate. For the gate is wide and the road is broad that leads to destruction, and there are many who go through it. How narrow is the gate and difficult the road that leads to life, and few find it (Matt. 7:3–14). Few find it! In fact, none will find it if we who know Jesus do not tell them. Here is our motivation for evangelism and missions.

What is amazing is that there is a way for sinners to be reconciled to God and go to heaven. That way is Jesus; He is all the way we need. And He is ready and willing to welcome all who come to Him in repentance and faith. Amazing grace!

The famed 15th century writer Thomas a Kempis is credited with writing these words that summarize this statement of Jesus:

> Without the Way we cannot go;
> Without the Truth we cannot know;
> Without the Life we cannot live.

Study Guide

B—(Basic truth about Jesus) Jesus is the way to God, the truth about God, and the life of God.

U—(Using the truth about Jesus) Compose a statement of gratitude to the Lord including the three claims made by Him in this study.

S—(Searching for more truth about Jesus) Jesus's claim to be the Way, the Truth, and the Life was given to Thomas in response to his question (John 14:5). Compare this with the events found in John 20:24–29. Have you made this discovery of who Jesus is?

H—(Honoring the truth about Jesus through prayer) Offer a prayer of praise to God that He provided in Jesus a way to Him, the truth about Him, and the life He came to give.

Chapter Twenty-Two

I Am the Vine

The basic purpose of the seventh and final I AM statement in John's Gospel is the same as the previous six. Jesus is revealing Himself by helping us understand who He is and what He wants to mean to us. Each illustration communicates a simple truth. A personal relationship with Jesus is absolutely essential for us to become the person God created us to be. As He clearly states in the passage before us, "You can do nothing without Me" (John 15:5).

Some biblical interpreters suggest that as Jesus and His disciples left the Upper Room (14:31), they may have passed a grape vineyard on their way to the Garden of Gethsemane. The sight of these vines may have given Jesus the occasion to make the statement: "I am the true vine, and my Father is the vineyard keeper . . . . I am the vine; you are the branches" (John 15:1, 5). Whether this suggestion is true or not, these men were very familiar with the process of growing grapes—a common practice in that area. They readily understood what Jesus was teaching through this example.

Look with me at four key words in this I AM claim of Jesus. First, the term "vine" is inclusive of the entire plant—root, stem, branches, leaves, and fruit. Jesus compared Himself to a fruitful plant. The Father ("the vineyard keeper") planted Him in this world to produce all that humankind needed to have an abundant, fruitful, eternal life. Jesus is the "true vine" as opposed to every other religious leader who claims to be God's appointed gift to the world.

The second term, "branches," describes all people who are genuine followers of Jesus—"you are the branches." The vine gives support and nourishment to the branches. If branches are cut off, they "can do nothing." Branches must remain firmly attached to the vine if they are to bear fruit. However, the vine needs the branches just as the branches need the vine. They are essential to one another and both are parts of the whole process.

"Remain" is the third significant word: "The one who remains in Me and I in him produces much fruit" (John 15:5). Some form of this Greek word is found eleven times in verses 1–11 of John 15. To remain in Christ means to have an intimate fellowship with Him continually and to live daily in communion with Him. Jesus explained what is required for this ongoing relationship to happen: "If you keep My commands you will remain in My love, just as I have kept My Father's commands and remain in His love" (v. 10). You may ask, "What commands?" His answer is clear: "This is My command: love one another as I have loved you … . This is what I command you: love one another" (vv. 12, 17). All the commands of God dealing with our relationships with others are summed up in one simple statement: "Love one another."

The fourth word, "fruit," completes the metaphor. As quoted above, "The one who remains in Me and I in him produces much fruit" (John 15:5). Grapevines are planted, cultivated, and pruned for one purpose—to produce grapes. In like manner, we are brought into a personal relationship with Christ for one primary purpose—to be fruitful. Notice a progression in Jesus's teaching here regarding fruit. First, He spoke of branches producing "fruit" (v. 2), then "more fruit" (v. 2), then "much fruit" (v. 5), and finally, "remaining fruit" (v. 16).

However, branches cannot produce fruit on their own. They are dependent on the vine to produce fruit. Branches simply carry the fruit-producing nourishment that comes up from the roots. This truth is the reason Jesus said, "without Me you can do nothing." Without a close, intimate, abiding connection to Jesus, no fruit will be produced on the branches.

Just what is this fruit? And how can we know if we are producing fruit? The best biblical answer to these questions is found in Paul's letter to the Galatians where he spoke of the "fruit of the Spirit." Here is his list of those virtues produced by the Holy Spirit in and through believers (branches): "The fruit of the Spirit is love, joy, peace, patience, kindness, goodness, faith, gentleness, self-control" (Gal. 5: 22–23). These nine terms actually describe the character of Jesus. Thus the fruit that Jesus, the Vine, produces through those who are intimately connected to Him is His own likeness!

The more our attitude, behavior, lifestyle, and character reflect the person of Jesus, the more fruitful we are being. Look back at His command. The more we love others as He loves us, the more His fruit is produced through us as His branches. As He said, without Him we cannot do this. We cannot of ourselves produce Christ's likeness. So like the branches of the vine, we must remain firmly in fellowship with Him.

We must not move beyond this subject without noting the stern words of warning Jesus gave. He spoke of His Father as the "vineyard keeper." The Father is committed to ensuring the health and productivity of the vine. This care includes removing unfruitful branches and pruning fruitful ones (John 15:2). The action of removing and burning branches that do not remain in the vine is not to be interpreted as depicting Christians becoming lost and perishing. The subject is not security but fruitfulness. Failing to "remain" in close fellowship with the vine will result in a barren, fruitless Christian life.

The process of pruning grapevines is for the purpose of increasing fruitfulness. This action refers to the Father's chastisement of believers in order to make them more productive. The pruning may at times seem severe and painful, but the result brings glory to the Father (John 15:8). The vine exists for the glory of the vineyard's keeper. The branches and their fruit play an essential role in this divine plan.

Now is an appropriate time for us to become "fruit inspectors," in the sense of examining ourselves. Is the fruit of the Spirit evident in us? Are we becoming progressively more fruitful? If not, we must expect, and welcome, the Father's pruning.

Study Guide

B—(Basic truth about Jesus) Fellowship with Jesus is essential for a productive life.

U—(Using the truth about Jesus) What are you doing to develop your fellowship with Jesus? How would you describe a fruitless Christian life?

S—(Searching for more truth about Jesus) Read 1 John 4-5. Write a summary of what is essential to having fellowship with Jesus.

H—(Honoring the truth about Jesus through prayer) For one week, begin each day by asking the Lord to produce more of His likeness through you.

Chapter Twenty-Three
I Am the Alpha and the Omega

We can now consider one final I AM claim. This title for Jesus is the most all-encompassing. The Lord's first words in Revelation are: "I am the Alpha and the Omega" (Rev. 1:8). Alpha is the first letter of the Greek alphabet; omega is the last. Some Bibles paraphrase this sentence to read, "I am A and Z." Later in Revelation 1, Jesus used these words: "I am the First and the Last" (v. 17). These claims then are combined in this statement: "I am the Alpha and Omega, the Beginning and End" (Rev. 21:6). Finally, all three affirmations occur: "I am the Alpha and Omega, the First and the Last, the Beginning and the End" (Rev. 22:13). Old Testament references to these terms include Isaiah 41:4, 44:6, and 48:12.

I heard a fine Bible teacher comment on these words and say, "Jesus is the beginning and the end, and everything in between!" Truly, He is the beginner and the ender. He was present in the very beginning as the Creator, He has been present throughout all history, and He will be present at the close. He is omnipresent. Not only is He omnipresent but also omnipotent—in complete control!

How does this truth affect us? What can we learn that is of practical significance from this amazing claim of Jesus? Consider these applications: First, we can have a sense of peace in knowing Who is in control of history. Yahweh chose to begin humankind, has always been sovereign over events, and will bring history to a planned conclusion in His own time. In this year of 2009, America is facing a severe financial crisis. Many good people have lost their jobs, houses, and much of their savings for retirement. Some citizens are paralyzed with a sense of fear. However, we who know the One who is the Alpha and the Omega find peace and security in Him. When tempted to panic, we remember that He is the same yesterday, today, and forever. As an old hymn reminds us, "Change and decay in all around I see, O Thou who changes not abide with me."

A second application is found in the word *mission*. In His sovereignty, Yahweh chose to bring you and me into this world at this particular time for His purpose. We are not here by accident. He is our personal Alpha and Omega—that is, He determined when our lives would begin and end in this world. The writer of Ecclesiastes declared, "There is … a time to give birth and a time to die …. He [God] has made everything appropriate in its time" (Eccl. 3:1–2, 11). The prophet Jeremiah adds further significance to this truth when he shares this message from Yahweh, "For I know the plans I have for you—this is the LORD's declaration—plans for your welfare, not for disaster, to give you a future and a hope" (Jer. 29:11).

We are Yahweh's people on His mission at His time in history. What personal importance this fact gives to each of us! Following His resurrection from the dead, Jesus said to His disciples, "Peace be to you! As the Father has sent Me, I also send you" (John 20:21). These words express His basic plan for each of us. We are a sent people, sent to fulfill His purpose for creating us. Our primary responsibility for this mission is to be fully available to Him today and every day. One Christian leader has observed that the Lord is looking for individuals who are willing to become a FAT FROG! This statement sounds weird until the acronym is explained: Faithful, Available, Teachable persons who will Fully Rely On God. Every day we must choose to follow this divine design.

A third practical application of knowing our Lord as the Alpha and Omega is expressed by the term *worship*. This statement is appropriate here: "Christian worship is the most momentous, the most urgent, the most glorious action that can take place in human life." Worship is an expression of value. We worship the person or object that we value most highly. In fact, the word *worship* is a contraction of worth-ship.

Our Lord, who is the Alpha and the Omega, is the only person worthy of our adoration and praise. He who is both the creator and sovereign ruler of all creation deserves our utmost devotion. Let us give priority to that which is priority—to worship Him with sincere and heartfelt gratitude in recognition of who He is. How instructive for us worshipers are the words of Jesus to the woman He encountered at a well in Samaria. He said, "An hour is coming and is now here, when the true worshipers will worship the Father in spirit and truth. Yes, the Father wants such people to worship Him" (John 4:23).

One part of John's vision as recorded in Revelation is a remarkable scene of worship: "Then I looked, and heard the voice of many angels around the throne, and also of the living creatures, and of the elders. Their number was countless thousands, plus thousands of thousands. They said with a loud voice: The Lamb who was slaughtered is worthy to receive power and riches And wisdom and strength and honor and glory and blessings! (Rev. 5:11-12).

Worthy is the Lamb! He who is the Lamb of God who takes away the sin of the world—He is worthy of our worship.

Now consider a final aspect of this amazing title of the Lord God, one that greatly enlarges the dimension of our lives. Look once again at His words, "'I am the Alpha and the Omega,' says the Lord God, 'the One who is, who was, and who is coming, the Almighty'" (Rev. 1:8). Humankind, apart from Jesus, is isolated—separated from the past and the future, as well as cut off from God in the present. But when He who is the beginning and the end and the present lives in us, we are thereby connected to the past, present, and future. What an amazing reality!

All past history becomes significant for us because we know "the One who was," who began all things and has controlled them. Moreover, we are connected to the future by our personal relationship to "the One who is coming," who includes us in His plans that are yet to be fulfilled. Most important of all, "the One who is" literally lives in us and we continually enjoy intimate fellowship with Him. From eternity past to eternity future, we are a part of His purpose. Awesome!

Study Guide

B—(Basic truth about Jesus) History begins and ends by the creation and control of Jesus.

U—(Using the truth about Jesus) List four applications of Jesus's claim to be the Alpha and the Omega.

S—(Searching for more truth about Jesus) Read the following biblical references: Isaiah 41:4, 44:6, and 48:12. What do you find in these verses regarding this title for Jesus?

H—(Honoring the truth about Jesus through prayer) Express your worship of the Lord based on the four applications listed in this chapter.

Conclusion

Yahweh is the name above all names. That name occurs 6,823 times in the Old Testament. Moreover, we have seen that the name *Jesus* has *Yahweh* as its Hebrew root. Add more than 900 New Testament occurrences of His name for a total in excess of 7,700! However, the frequency of this name is not the most significant factor. The meaning of *Yahweh* is what arrests our attention and deserves our appreciation.

Listen to this profound insight from Julie Ackerman Link in *Our Daily Bread:* "A sentence needs only two things to be complete: a subject and a verb. So when God says His name is 'I AM,' it conveys the concept that He is complete in Himself. He is subject and verb. He is everything we could possibly need." He has expressed this powerful truth more than 7,700 times in His Word. This fact is the reason that we must insist on knowing and referring to Him by His name Yahweh, which means I AM, not Jehovah, which has no meaning, and not LORD, which is His title but not His name.

I AM

I was regretting the past and fearing the future.
Suddenly, my Lord was speaking.
My name is I am. He paused.
I waited. He continued.

When you live in the past with
Its mistakes and regrets
It is hard. I am not there.
My name is not I Was.

When you live in the future
With its problems and fears
It is hard. I am not there.
My name is not I Will Be.

When you live in this moment
It is not hard. I am here.
My name is I AM.

By Helen Mallicost

One final appeal in these words of Psalm 34:3:

"Proclaim with me YAHWEH's greatness; let us exalt His name together."

Bibliography

Arthur, Kay. *Lord, I Want to Know You.* Old Tappan, NJ: Fleming H. Revell Co. 1984.

Goard, Wm. Pascoe. *The Names of God.* Muskogee, OK: Hoffman Printing Co. 2001.

Lockyer, Herbert. *All the Divine Names and Titles in the Bible.* Grand Rapids: Zondervan, 1975.

Morgan, Robert J. *He Shall Be Called.* New York: Warner Faith, 2005

Spangler, Ann. *Praying the Names of God.* Grand Rapids: Zondervan, 2004.

Stevenson, Herbert F. *Titles of the Triune God.* Greenwood, IN: Capstone Books, 2004.

Stone, Nathan. *Names of God.* Chicago: Moody Press, 1944.

Weisman, Charles A. *The Sacred Names Issue.* Apple Valley, MN: Weisman Publications, 2006

Wiersbe, Warren W. *The Wonderful Names of Jesus.* Wheaton, IL: Victor Books, 1980.

Commentaries, Dictionary, and Handbook Consulted:

Allen, Clifton J., ed. *The Broadman Bible Commentary*. 12 vols. Nashville: Broadman Press, 1969.

Butler, Trent C., ed. *Holman Illustrated Bible Dictionary*. Nashville:Holman Bible Publishers, 2003

Clendenen, Ray E., ed. *The New American Commentary*, 38 vols. Nashville:Broadman & Holman Publishers, 2003.

Dockery, David S., ed. *Holman Bible Handbook*. Nashville: Holman Bible Publishers, 1992

Gaebelein, Frank E., ed. *The Expositor's Bible Commentary*. 12 vols. Grand Rapids: The Zondervan Corp., 1979.

Wiersbe, Warren W., *The Bible Exposition Commentary*. 2 vols. Colorado Springs: Chariot Victor Publishing, 1989.